The Cottages of

LILLIPUT LANE

PARVA SUNT PULCHRA

'Saxham St. Edmunds is our celebration of the tranquility and timelessness of rural England. Ours is a world of pink limewashed plaster, well-worn brick and tile, and weathered oak. The cottages merge into the East Anglian landscape where trees dwarf the buildings, creepers reach skywards and herbaceous borders flourish in the Suffolk countryside. Where the people and their homes are such an integral part, and the village green, the focal point of their lives. Inspired by the villages of Cavendish and Bungay our village would be found in East Anglia in the South East of England.'

—David J. Tate

The Cottages of

LILLIPUT LANE

Photography by Walter Pfeiffer

Text by Deborah Scott

A Robert Campbell Rowe Book
Portfolio Press
Huntington, New York

CONTENTS

Gamekeepers Cottage

Covered Bridge   *Forge Barn*

Old Mine

FOUNDER'S INTRODUCTION

*S*ince the first day that Lilliput Lane was formed, my life has changed

enormously, but the principles on which the company was founded have not

changed at all. I set out to create an environment of fun and challenge, a

democratic company working collectively in a caring, honest and unselfish

way. Many people throughout those early years have made individual

contributions to the company's success and have moved on, but as I look

around me today, I see scores of successful 'Lilliputians' who enjoy their work every day, with an energy and commitment to which many others can only aspire.

As a simple means of making a living, we set out to encapsulate and preserve the work of our forefathers for posterity and for the enrichment of this ever-changing world. We did not realise at the time just how many tens of thousands of people shared our love of this country's unique architectural heritage. We have,

intentionally and sometimes almost by accident, raised public awareness of the very existence of vernacular architecture as a signpost to the geography and social history of this great nation.

We could not have achieved the goals we set without the support of our staff, each and every member, who understand the importance of quality in everything they do; always changing, evolving and improving throughout the years. Every production employee understands how the product they produce is the ultimate test of the company's worth and that you the collector judge us all by the product you

hold in your hand. Development of systems and designs will continue apace in the next ten years as they have in the past, providing an unrivalled quality of product and service to our valued customers.

As I reflect now on the many accolades and achievements and the hard work I and many others have put in to create this success, I would like to recognise the support I have received from many, particularly my wife Sandra and our girls — without whose unfailing support I could realise no hope or ambition — and my mother, from whom I inherited a stubborness and a tenacity that knows no such failure, only opportunity.

But I would like to thank you, the collectors, around the world, for the part you play in ensuring the future not only of our cottage heritage, but also of the dedicated band of people, whose care, integrity and sheer hard work make today's Lilliput Lane collection possible.

David John Tate, MBE
Cumbria, England
July 1991

Dow

A His

Lilliput Lane

Early Days: The original inspiration for Lilliput Lane and its remarkable range of models was the vernacular architecture of Britain — in particular, the cottages that give the British countryside the character and charm that enchant visitors from all over the world. Lilliput Lane's founder, artist and Technical Director, David Tate, describes vernacular architecture as 'the buildings built by the

people for the people with the materials that lay around them.' It was his enduring passion for these humble yet delightful dwellings that was eventually to find expression in the countless exquisite models produced at Lilliput.

David Tate is a Yorkshireman, and has the strong passions, direct manner and determination for which his countrymen are renowned, along with a ready sense of humour. The passion is clear when he talks of the cottages he loves, and the success of Lilliput Lane is attributable in no small part to his determination, tenacity and sheer energy. Born in the unromantic surroundings of one of Yorkshire's industrial mill towns, Tate experienced early on in life a yearning to escape to the countryside. This urge found expression not only in his love of outdoor sports

— canoeing, walking and mountaineering — but also in a captivation with the landscape itself and its characteristic buildings.

With a proven artistic talent by the age of ten (he was painting, drawing and sculpting by then and even earning pocket money from selling his work), it is not surprising that he had an acute visual memory that made him highly observant. Long childhood journeys down from Yorkshire to visit his aunt in Bedford showed him the architecture of the countryside as he travelled southwards. He observed the contrasts, remembering the thatched cottages of Bedfordshire, their styles and colours, and remarking on how different they were to the windswept houses of the north. Thus started his lifelong romance with the vernacular.

The search for adventure and escape, along with a natural talent for leadership, led Tate to a career in the army, where he took full advantage of the many opportunities it offers. When he was not beating a path through the forests of Malaysia, he was discovering about engineering, and developing extensive knowledge of fibreglass moulding and its potential. On coming out of the army, he applied the technical skills he had acquired to industry, and his proud boast was that he could make a mould for anything, proving it by making in fibreglass everything from a canoe to a pantomime egg. Before long he set up his own company in Hampshire, working as a designer, consultant and sculptor.

In the course of this work, he developed a revolutionary new system of moulding, which allowed small, intricate objects to be moulded in one piece — a great advance on the more time-consuming process of moulding in several pieces and reassembling. The key to his innovative system was that the original master copy of the sculpted wax model could be cast in one piece with its base, which allowed thinner moulds to be made repeatedly. The advantages of this were manifold, but most significantly it meant that much finer detail could be cast than before, and it also made production easier and faster. David Tate's extensive knowledge of the nature of the silicone elastomers used for the moulds was critical to the success of this system, allowing him to create moulds that held infinitely fine detail yet remained flexible enough to be easily removed. The obvious potential of this system made him realise that he might at last

11

Plate 57. Blaise Hamlet, Vine Cottage: south-west elevation and chamber plan, from the *Pavilion Notebook*. The gable end with pigeon holes is responded to by the same device at Double Cottage. One ... to emphasise the major axis of Nash's plan, One

be able to bring a long-held dream of his to fruition.

'In the process of earning my living I wanted to combine all the things that make life enjoyable — sunshine, fun, cottages, countryside and youth,' recalls David. 'Above all else, I enjoy the creative process, and here I felt was a chance to develop something magical, taking time and care to share with people something that was really good, that truly represented value for money at a time when, in so many areas, greed was getting the

better of quality.' He started to make plans to move to the Lake District (which he knew and loved, being a keen climber) and set up a business there that would use his innovative moulding system to produce models of cottages. People had made models of cottage for many years, but these would be different in that they would be closely influenced by authentic vernacular architecture, not by fantasy of imagination. David Tate sculpted fourteen models, some local to the Lake District

Exports go to U.S.

22-10-83

MOVE TO PENRITH LED TO SUCCESS FOR MODEL MAKERS

A FIRM producing ornamental miniature buildings at Penrith has taken huge strides forward in its first year.

Lilliput Lane Ltd. set out with a staff of six last Autumn. Now they have 44 and say that, with home and export markets blossoming, there is every prospect of another twenty jobs being created within the next year.

"It has developed even better than we expected," said David Tate, the firm's sculptor and co-founder.

He and managing director Tony Barnes moved to Penrith from the South of England to establish their venture, with the conviction that they could produce better models of character buildings than those already on the market.

They were also looking for a pleasant part of the country to work in and chose Skirsgill Park, on the outskirts of Penrith, where Mr. Anthony Leeming has converted a range of 18th Century estate buildings into light industrial premises.

At first the firm took 350 square feet of space, but now occupy 8,000 square feet!

PROJECTIONS

The first year's turnover has topped £200,000 and projections indicate £500,000 in

Australia and the Caribbean. Negotiations are currently in progress for sales in Canada, New Zealand, Japan, Spain and the Canary Islands.

"It was very much hand-to-mouth when we started, but we were very determined and then the market place exploded and the expansion came," said Mr. Tate.

"However, we have been very careful to do it on the right financial lines. We took stock after six months and consulted the bank manager and accountant for advice and we have done the same thing again after completing the first year.

"The third year is often the critical one for a business venture and we want to make sure of making it through that," added Mr. Tate.

More than fifty British firms produce model buildings, but Lilliput Lane says that only they and one other

Directors believe that staff respond to a good working environment and by next Summer the firm plans to have a small fleet of company canoes and fibreglass boats which the workers can use.

"We want people to come to work, enjoy themselves, be interested in what they do and feel they are involved," said Mr. Tate.

Monique Baggerman, from Penrith, is a supervisor in charge of a dozen girls in the painting department.

"It is a very good firm to work for because they look after the staff," she said. "The atmosphere and relationships are completely different from my previous job in which I worked for eight years in an office."

Lilliput Lane directors David Tate a

and Yorkshire (Dale Farm, Dale House and Lakeside House), others from farther afield (The Croft, Drapers and The Old Post Office, amongst others). The first one he ever sculpted for Lilliput was Dale House, followed by Honeysuckle and April Cottage, models that were to enjoy long-lived popularity.

So strong was his conviction, that he sold his house and nearly all his possessions to raise some capital to get started. To risk everything in such a way showed true Yorkshire grit, but David makes little of it. 'I never doubted for a second it would succeed,' he says. He set about finding premises where he could set up his mould-making system and get on with production. His choice was limited by the fact that he also needed a home for his wife Sandra and their two teenage daughters, Jeanette and Deborah, so industrial sites were hardly suitable. Finally, in the late summer of 1982, he found the old stables belonging to Skirsgill, a fine, late 18th-century, red sandstone mansion just outside Penrith in Cumbria. The owner had converted them into 'units', which were available to rent to small businesses, and David Tate accordingly rented a couple of workshops totalling 800 square feet. Into the bargain came Rose Cottage, a tiny, Spartan cottage in what had been the farmyard, where David and his family came to live in September 1982. Lilliput Lane was launched.

Not everyone was thrilled by the move. Jeanette and Deborah Tate were sixteen and seventeen respectively, and loathe to leave their friends in the South. Nonetheless, the whole family put their backs into the production of David's four-teen models, working eighteen hours a day, seven days a week, and retiring to sleep in the primitive, damp cottage, otherwise known, less than affectionately,

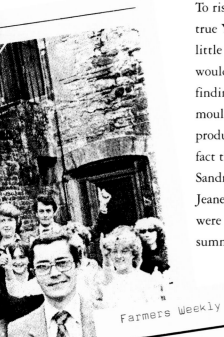

Barnes with many me

Farmers Weekly   21 October 1983

Lane full of great little houses

A COTTAGE industry in more ways than one — that's Lilliput Lane.

For the company which takes its name from Daniel Defoe's famous book *Gulliver's Travels*, specialises in producing exquisite-ly miniaturised English houses and cottages in minute detail — though there is nothing small about its success.

Started in September 1982, the company was the brain-child of two men. Antony Barnes and David Tate. Antony's business experience in the pottery trade and David's expertise as a sculptor led them from jobs in the south to set up on their own in d buildings belonging to

a Cornish village post office and a 16th century Surrey farmhouse, and the superbly re-created Castle Street based on a medieval town of northern England.

Other more expensive pieces in-clude Warwick Hall, described as "a fanciful farmer's residence typical of the Vale of Cheshire and West Midlands with oak beams and close studding."

Each property to be reproduced is first visited, photographed, drawn and extensively researched before work begins on creating a sculpted wax model from which the master mould is made.

Already UK demand is nation-wide and orders from America, New Zealand and Australia are pouring in.

"I think the big attraction of

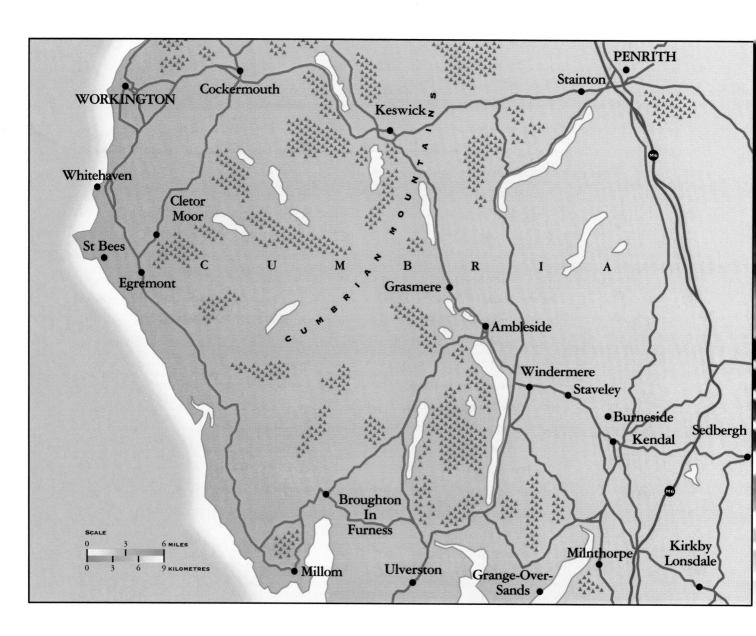

PENRITH

Stainton

WORKINGTON

Cockermouth

Keswick

Whitehaven

Cletor
Moor

St Bees

Egremont

C U M B R I A

CUMBRIAN MOUNTAINS

Grasmere

Ambleside

Windermere
Staveley

Burneside
Kendal

Sedbergh

Broughton
In
Furness

Millom

Ulverston

Grange-Over-
Sands

Milnthorpe

Kirkby
Lonsdale

SCALE

0   3   6 MILES

0   3   6   9 KILOMETRES

M6

as 'the swamp'. The prospects for comfortable sleep were further eroded when David dismantled the pine bed, using the planking to make badly needed painting tables. The original workshops were the rooms that now form the Research and Development office, and in this confined area every aspect of production from mould-making to painting had to be carried out.

From September until after Christmas in 1982, the Tate family (and four other colleagues) barely stopped to draw breath. Jeanette Tate recalls, 'I was in charge of mould-making with Dad, and Mum did the casting. There was no-one to take on staff and train painters, so I was doing that as well. At the beginning, we did our own jobs during the day, then painted from about seven until midnight. I also used to write the label stickers myself by hand the first two or three months until we had them printed.' Four more models (mostly of local origin) were introduced in November (Bridge House, Burnside, Castle Street and Holly Cottage), bringing the range to eighteen.

The materials that were used in those early days were far less sophisticated than today's. Models were cast in a very basic 'Crystacal' plaster, which was light in weight and bright white in colour. It was difficult to mix consistently, and this created problems since the amount of water in the plaster affected the way the paint went on, altering its intensity.

The paints themselves were newly developed by Tate from dyes suspended in shellac and methylated spirit. The use of dyes rather than the conventional ground-up paint pigments offered brighter colours. However, the system was still vulnerable to the quality of supplies, and early on they were alarmed to discover that the colours they had been sent were not light-fast, fading in bright sunshine. The models were swiftly recalled, and all the supplies in the cupboards were thrown out while David once more worked out the complex formulae essential for colour consistency, using a new range of dyes. Such decisive action was typical of the emerging company attitude — always striving to improve and not afraid to take bold, innovative steps in order to do so.

Within three weeks of starting up, the company had cottages to sell, and

David Tate out for a climb in the Lake District.

Company headquarters shown in a 1984 photograph.

Deborah Tate took them to shops in the local Lake District area, first finding success at Mrs Stephen's Giftshop in Keswick. The retailers were cautious at first, but Christmas proved to them that Lilliput Lane's cottages had special qualities that appealed to customers. It seemed that the magic that had captivated David Tate evoked a similar response amongst others too. Whether because of nostalgia, historical interest, or just through their own charm, the cottages were meeting with enthusiastic support. Early in the new year the retailers began to reorder, much to the delight of the tiny but expanding work force at Skirsgill.

Ten more cottages were introduced in time for the Birmingham gift fair in February, and orders increased. Meanwhile, improvements were constantly being made, one of the most important being the introduction of glass-reinforced plastic (GRP) cases to the mould-making process, replacing the previous plaster cases. The significance of this improvement was that it stopped the shrinkage of models, which

was an inherent problem of the original system and had resulted in models becoming smaller and smaller over a period. GRP also improved the quality of moulds and allowed more complex pieces to be made, while extending the life of each mould — an important factor in costings. These improvements meant that it was worth reworking some of the original models that suffered from shrinkage, including Acorn Cottage (reworked September 1983) and April Cottage (reworked July 1984).

Within a few months of starting, Lilliput Lane was employing its first full-time sales person, Gail Tuck, a native Cumbrian. Her brief was to go out and get the cottages into shops all over the country, so she took to the road in her company car, a vehicle of such age and chequered experience that she describes it as 'dimpled'.

Gail Tuck recalls how impressed she was with the cottages then. 'To me they looked fantastic. Although they were nowhere near today's exacting standards, their good quality stood out, and there was nothing quite like them. Yet they offered real value for money at a price anyone could afford — the range was around £2.50–£20 at that time.' Though she experienced some initial resistance from a few of the most traditional and reactionary glass and china retailers, most were happy to give it a try once they saw the quality of Lilliput Lane's products. At first they would take perhaps five or six models, but as these began to sell, the retailers would take more.

Gail Tuck's duties were rather broader than sales at that early stage, however. Such were the cash flow problems (inherent in any small but expanding business) that she would frequently find herself driving straight from a retailer to a supplier, using whatever cash she had managed to raise through sales to buy desperately needed raw materials for the next day's production. She would also divert via the local supermarket to scavenge for empty cardboard boxes so that she had something to pack the cottages in for delivery. The company workers were at this stage handmaking individual boxes for the cottages, but they had no time or money for delivery crates.

These cash flow problems also meant that before long there was no-one in the company who had not been stranded in their car, having run out of petrol through lack of funds. Notwithstanding such difficulties, when Gail Tuck triumphantly brought back the first £100 order, David Tate took everyone out to supper to celebrate (although the bill came to more than the order). This familial and collective attitude characterised Lilliput Lane as a company, and its closeness has endured throughout considerable expansion, against all the normal odds.

Anne Woods and John Shapiro at work in what is now the Accounts Department.

18 *Sue Barnes, top and centre, the first full-time sales rep. In the lower picture, the woman in the middle, Marjorie Dalton, is still with the company after nine years.*

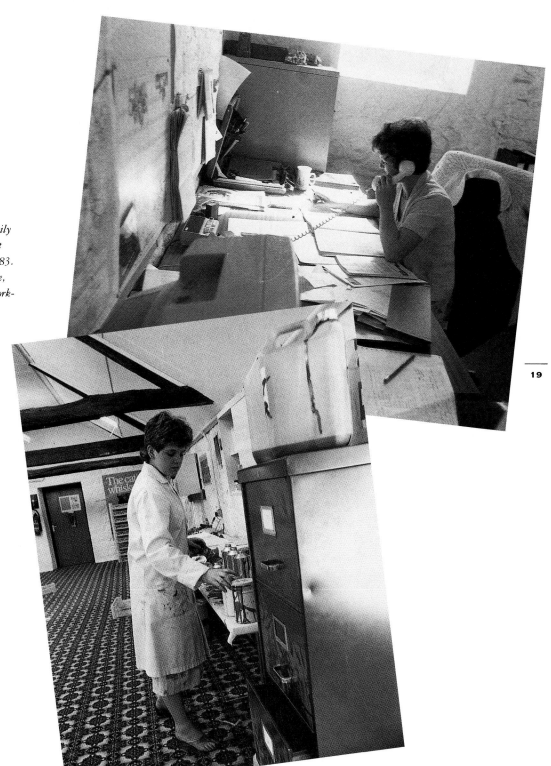

Members of the Tate family at work. Top, Sandra at the front desk early in 1983. Below, daughter Jeanette, seen in the early days working in the studio.

19

DEVELOPMENT AND EXPANSION

Despite the success with which the cottages were met in the marketplace, the first three years were a difficult time for Lilliput Lane, which lacked the funding necessary to take full advantage of this growing popularity. Nonetheless, the company did begin to expand, taking on more staff and spreading from the original workshops to take over more and more of the farmyard buildings, eventually ousting 7,500 chickens to make room for the painters.

Two major technical developments were introduced towards the end of 1984 that were to have long-lasting effects. The first concerned the paint system. The

summer periods had proved that the spirit base used for the colours was not ideal because it tended to evaporate, subtly concentrating and therefore darkening the colour and making it thicker. Close scrutiny showed that, over a period, the colours used on the models were thus becoming darker, and that the detail was becoming obscured by the thicker paint. David Tate spent a long period experimenting with water-based paints, finally arriving at a system that employed earth-based pigments in a water/polymer base. The resulting colours had a transparency that made them more like washes and allowed the detail to show up far better than before. Clare Cottage and the other

David Tate explains the process to then Deputy Prime Minister William Whitelaw, who is now Lord Whitelaw.

models introduced in February 1985 were the first to benefit from this system.

The second development concerned the plaster from which the models were cast. The original plaster was not ideal, being light in weight and fragile. David Tate worked out a specification for the properties he required of the plaster — from viscosity (important in the moulding of detail) to final hardness — and the result was Amorphite. Amorphite has unique properties that make it ideal for casting the models that Lilliput Lane makes: It is very hard and durable; it is fine enough to portray the most minute sculptural detail, and it is workable in production. The Amorphite has proved so successful, there have been only the most minor adjustments to it since.

With these two advances Lilliput Lane was far better equipped to grow and develop the market it had already established. By the summer of 1985, the number of models in production was approaching fifty, and some sixty people were employed by the company. A major change in management occurred in July 1985 that was to revolutionise the company and signal the start of a period of heady growth. William Dodd, who had joined Lilliput Lane by this time as Chairman, made a contribution of critical importance at this point. His background as an accountant and his business-like approach enabled him to establish the company on a sound financial footing, helping it to develop its full potential.

The effect of this change was that the immediate and paralysing constraints of

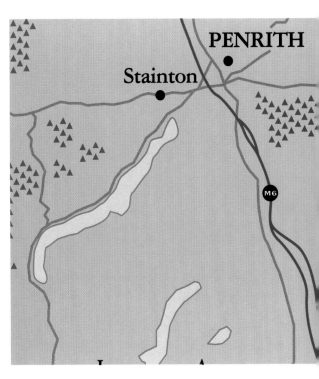

cost, which had hitherto cramped progress and caused everything to be done in the minimum time, were removed. Sculpting could now take the time required to perfect pieces, and the tooling process, so crucial to successful production, also benefited. The rewards of this release of pressure were immediately apparent in the models. Kentish Oast and Watermill, introduced in July 1985, both show unprecedented detail that bears testament to the additional time and care that were put into them. The former, with its 7,500 individually placed tiles, and the latter, featuring the miller inside the doorway, marked the introduction of the idiosyncratic detail that enhances the credibility of Lilliput Lane models and has endeared them to such a wide collectorship.

There followed a period of rapid expansion during which, as David Tate

21

recalls, 'The company really took off, increasing productivity and profitability, and introducing the cottages to new marketplaces. Nothing was too great a challenge.' As well as developing the home market, Lilliput Lane had found representatives in the United States — originally the Kellogg Company and, from 1985, the Schmid Corporation — which introduced the cottages to a trans-Atlantic audience for the first time. A new range of pieces were specially sculpted for the North American market, including the Log Cabin and the Adobe Village.

The root of this burgeoning success was the popularity of the Lilliput Lane cottages in the marketplace. But who was buying them? Initially David Tate had envisaged that they would be bought as gifts or perhaps mementos of a holiday or childhood memory of such cottages. Towards the end of 1985, the management at Lilliput Lane became aware that the cottages were not just being bought as 'one-off' purchases, but that many people were collecting them in earnest. The number of enquiries the company was receiving from these collectors was growing rapidly, and evidence of their enthusiasm was also experienced by the painters whenever they did a demonstration at a store.

True to its form as a company that thrives on involvement and participation, in the spring of 1986 it launched the Lilliput Lane Collectors' Club. In the first month nearly 500 people joined, keen to enjoy the benefits offered, including invitations to demonstrations, the opportunity to buy special-edition cottages exclusive to members and their own newsletter, *Gul-*

liver's World. On joining, each member was also sent a free gift, the 'Pack Horse Bridge', the first of a series of annual Collectors' Club gifts for joining and renewing members. This marked the beginning of a happy bond between the collectors and the company that was to bring great mutual enjoyment and benefit to both and become an essential factor in the success of Lilliput Lane. The feedback from the collectors offered invaluable information to a company dedicated to continual improvement of its products.

Awareness of Lilliput Lane was growing apace. Even the then Prime Minister, Mrs Margaret Thatcher, owned a cottage, named, perhaps prophetically, Thatcher's Rest. With awareness came burgeoning demand, which meant that more painters were needed. There was no more space available on the Penrith site at Skirsgill, so the management had to look elsewhere to set up new studios. In September 1986, they opened a new 10,000 sq ft manufacturing unit in Cockermouth, a market town in the west of the county. By December there were 100 painters working at Cockermouth, devolving the work on existing models from Penrith, allowing the latter to concentrate on new ranges. And with eleven new models introduced in 1986, and a further twelve launched at the International Spring Fair in Birmingham in 1987, there was plenty to do.

Another significant technical change took place in 1986, with the first piece specially made in a limited edition for the Collectors' Club members. David Tate wanted to give Crendon Manor a proper English garden, but the translucent paints

Two views of a Cumbrian building that inspired Troutbeck Farm.

could not capture the brilliance necessary for flower colours. He therefore developed a new technique for painting flowers, using an old painter's trick he had learned years before. By painting the flowers twice, initially with opaque white, and then with a colour wash, spectacular vivid shades were achieved that brought Crendon Manor's garden to life. This started Lilliput Lane on the theme of gardens, which it developed over the following years, making them just as important as the houses themselves.

With a foot already in America, Lilliput Lane had already shown its awareness of the foreign market. Keen to push the boundaries also into Europe, David Tate and his colleague, sculptor Tom Raine, set about learning to speak German, and undertook a 2,500 mile drive, researching Germany and Austria. The fruit of their labour, the German Collection, was launched in February 1987. The German and American collections were made available only in those countries respectively. Though these initial forays into the wider international market could not rival the success at home, they generated enough interest to encourage the management to plan future development, newly aware that the Lilliput Lane principle of representing local architecture in miniature did not appeal only to the British.

Further studios were opened in Workington on the west coast of Cumbria in May 1987, and rapidly took on over 150 people. Here every process of production could be carried out (from casting to painting to packing), helping to relieve the pressure on Penrith. Workington contributed to the production of the general range, as well as being sole producer of the newly introduced 'tinies' (cottages on an even smaller scale for low budget and starter collectors) and a number of other models.

By the company's fifth anniversary that autumn, there was plenty to celebrate, and in true style, the management threw a party for all its employees — no mean undertaking with over 500 of them, counting Penrith, Cockermouth and Workington. Tribute was paid to the work force by Chairman William Dodd and founder David Tate, emphasising the importance of each and every member of the company. Nor were the collectors forgotten in this celebration, for David Tate remarked that in his opinion there were no less than 8,500 members of the Lilliput Company, counting in the 8,000 collectors in the club. Praise came from outside too, with a message from David McLean, MP for Penrith and the Borders, calling Lilliput Lane 'Cumbria's fastest growing young company.'

Former chairman, Bill Dodd.

Former Prime Minister Margaret Thatcher with David McLean, Member of Parliament representing the Penrith area.

Having already garnered accolades such as the Cumbria County Export Award for 1987, and twice been a finalist in the CBI's prestigious 'Company of the Year' award, even greater honours were in the offing. In the New Year's Honours of 1988, David Tate was awarded the MBE in recognition of his achievements. Typically, he was quick to share the tribute with the staff at Lilliput Lane, to whose hard work he put down the success of the company. In the spring he attended a ceremony at Buckingham Palace where he received the honour from the Queen.

American readers may not be aware that the M.B.E. — Member of the Order of the British Empire — is a special distinction awarded to approximately 50 individuals each year in a special ceremony at Buckingham Palace presided over by the reigning monarch.

Meanwhile, Lilliput Lane was launch-ing its own American distribution subsidi-ary, Gift Link, based in Columbia, Mary-land, under the guidance of former UK Sales Director, Roger Fitness. Responding to the demand and potential of the exten-sive American market, Gift Link was to supply quality giftware shops and depart-ment stores throughout the United States, making the full range of Lilliput Lane's cottages available to the American public on a much wider scale. Concurrent with the opening of Gift Link, an American Collector's Club was launched to bring the benefits of membership to this enthusias-tic group of collectors. Within three months of Gift Link's opening, the man-agement's faith in the American market was given a tremendous boost at the world's biggest collectables fair in South Bend, Indiana, where Lilliput Lane's stand was besieged by thousands of eager collectors.

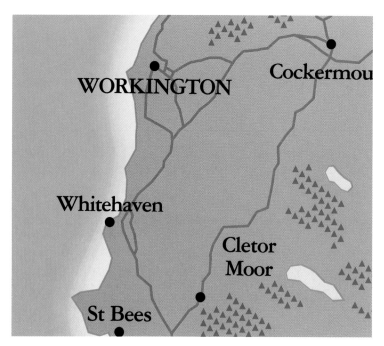

WORKINGTON

Cockermou

Whitehaven

Cletor
Moor

St Bees

By mid-1988, Lilliput Lane cottages could not only be bought in the United States but all over the world — in Australia, New Zealand, Canada and many European countries too. Such success brought the company another honour, when in September 1988 Lilliput Lane received the Queen's Award for Export and Achievement from the Lord Lieutenant of Cumbria, Sir Charles Graham. Again the honour was shared, with three staff members chosen to represent the company at a reception for the winners on board the Royal Yacht Britannia, where they were introduced to the Queen.

The introduction of new ranges had continued apace, with forty new models introduced in 1987, including Yew Tree

LILLIPUT Lane. — Private collector wishes to purchase Drapers or Miners Cottage. —

LILLIPUT Lane early models required. —

Farm, David Tate's own home, Street Scenes and the 'tinies' to encourage new collectors. The next year brought the range of Olde English Country Pubs, amongst a number of other cottages from around England, with 1988 culminating in the company's first Christmas piece, the seasonally snowy Deer Hall Park.

Lilliput Lane had come a long way from those first fourteen cottages that David Tate had sculpted six years earlier. By the end of 1988, there were more than sixty-eight different models in production, quite apart from the 'Land of Legend' fantasy range the company had also launched. Confidence was running high, and never satisfied to mark time, in 1989 the management at Lilliput Lane added more than forty new models to the range, breaking new ground in a number of areas. The introduction of a series of cottages inspired by Blaise Hamlet, the village designed and built by Regency architect John Nash, took Lilliput Lane for the first time into the area of 'Picturesque Architecture', a phenomenon of the 19th century when it was fashionable to build pretty cottages inspired by the vernacular architecture of previous centuries.

Perhaps most remarkable of the innovations that year was St Peter's Cove. At a height of eight inches, easily the largest and most ambitious model Lilliput Lane had ever made, it was a *tour de force* not only of sculpting but also of moulding technique. Comprising no less than ten different buildings all perched together on a steep hill overlooking a harbour, St Peter's Cove was based on an English village, typical of those on the South Coast and the Isle of Wight. The intricacy of detail, from the boats on the foreshore to the clock on the church, made this a remarkable achievement. Not surprisingly it was also the most expensive piece ever offered, and the management could not help but wonder how collectors would react to a price many times more than

people, but not ignoring the less romantic dwellings like the Stockwell Tenement, and the country churches of Ireland that serve as such a central focus of that country. The forbidding grandeur of Scottish castles like Craigievar, Claypotts and magnificent Blair Atholl broke new ground for Lilliput Lane, for the first time capturing

Staff party in 1987.

their usual outlay for a single cottage. They need not have worried. The limited edition of 3,000, scheduled to be spread over the following three years, was sold out within six months, collectors being happily prepared to wait a year or two for such a magnificent piece.

As if such innovations were not enough for one year, 1989 also saw the launch of both the Scottish and the Irish collections. Both were wide-ranging, capturing in miniature the enchanting thatched or stone-built homes of ordinary

buildings of monumental proportions on a miniature scale. Early in 1990, seven more Scottish homes were added to the range, from castles (Cawdor and Eilean Donan) to cottages like the Hebridean Hame and the Fisherman's Bothy.

On the international front, new ground was also broken, with the introduction of the 'American Landmarks' collection at the Indiana Collectables Exposition in July 1989. This was highly significant, bringing to Lilliput Lane's growing number of American collectors the chance to enjoy their own, unique architectural heritage. Well-known American artist Ray Day was invited by David Tate to sculpt these models, and they chose for the first four the Country Church, the Falls Mill, and the all-American Countryside Barn and Mail Pouch Barn. With the support of the dynamic Gift Link team, these enjoyed a successful launch in America and were followed in March by another eight models, capturing further rural landmarks of the heart of America.

Back in Cumbria, the increased demand meant that a new purpose built unit had been created at Workington and opened in spring 1989, replacing the old studios, allowing room to increase production and raising the number of casters to nearer a hundred. At the same time, another site was developed at Cleator Moor, an old

In 1988, Roger Fitness moved to America to open the company's own distribution organisation, Gift Link, Inc., in Columbia, Maryland.

Cumbrian pit town. This was initially destined to produce a new Lilliput Lane — the wall plaques, introduced to allow collectors with limited space to continue collecting. Starting with just five painters, a packer and a cleaner, Cleator Moor soon expanded to full production and took on not only a wider range of models but enough staff to bring the total employed by Lilliput Lane to around 650.

Never prepared to settle for the status quo, Lilliput Lane made more radical innovations in 1990. This was dubbed the year of the garden, and David Tate's own burgeoning interest in gardening made him determined that Lilliput Lane's gardens would be better than ever. The sculptors were all encouraged to read gardening books, so that they could not only study the plant forms, but also make sure that they chose to depict species that did in fact have concurrent flowering times, keeping up Lilliput Lane's reputation for meticulous authenticity. The sculptors also learnt to sculpt each flower and leaf individually, a skill requiring all their remarkable patience, yet resulting in superb, life-like blooms that made the gardens an art form in themselves.

Once cast, every model is dipped in a translucent wash that imparts to it the colour of stone, and this is the basis to which the painters add the other colours. Another of the innovations in 1990 was the development of a new dip, which bit into the surface of the Amorphite, emphasising every detail more dramatically than ever before. Having brought out the detail so successfully, it then seemed a pity to

PM HEARS OF PENRITH 'MODEL OF SUCCESS'

MRS. Thatcher has had a first-hand account of the success story of Lilliput Lane, the Penrith-based model making company.

The Prime Minister was attending the launch of an "Enterprise Works" campaign in the new London Docklands arena, at which the work of the West Cumbria Development Agency was highlighted.

Lilliput Lane was one of just three companies to be interviewed at the launch by TV announcer Jan Leeming, who hosted the event.

Founder and technical director David Tate told her of Lilliput Lane's expansion from the original factory at Penrith, through to Cockermouth, Workington and Cleator Moor.

Later in the day, Mr. Tate had the opportunity to tell the Prime Minister of Lilliput Lane's progress, so that it now employs around 800 people.

Mrs. Thatcher expressed her "delight" with the company's success before cutting a large cake to celebrate ten years of the Enterprize Agency Movement.

AMERICAN MOVE

Lilliput Lane products also proved popular amongst the high flyers on an Oxfordshire Air Base, last weekend.

In the largest giftware demonstration ever held on an American Air Base, Lilliput Lane attracted more than three thousand US Airmen and their families.

The open weekend was attended by Mr. Tate, senior sculptor Ted Slack, and other representatives of the company.

According to sales director Andrew Dunning, interest among the Airmen and their families was intense.

He said: "The response to the event was terrific. Many of the people there were committed collectors of Lilliput Lane.

"Almost all the people who came to visit were on short two-year commissions in the United Kingdom so they will take their collections home when they return to the US or elsewhere. We are actively ensuring that they will be able to continue collecting our cottages wherever they go."

A look into Lilliput Lane

LEADING Penrith-based giftware manufacturers Lilliput Lane are holding a major summer fair at Greystoke Castle, Greystoke, on Sunday.

Visitors will have an opportunity to see the delicate art of painting a Lilliput Lane cottage, as well as having a chance to "paint their own" and meet sculptors and artists.

There will be attractions for all the family, including old English entertainment, musicians, acrobats, country dancing and a display of falconry.

Hodgson's of Carlisle will be running a shop at the fair, with the full range of Lilliput Lane pieces.

There will be a display of dry stone walling, the art of thatching and the country profession of spinning.

A proportion of proceeds from the event will be used to help restore the Castle and grounds to their former glories.

---

risk concealing it with paints, so the paint system once more came under scrutiny. All the paints were reformulated, making them more transparent and brighter. Once applied over the new dip, the effect was electric. The first pieces produced in the new colours found great popularity, and the management decided to apply this new system gradually to more and more of the range.

As if these changes were not enough for one year, a radical new system was also introduced into tool-making (the process by which the tools are created, from which repeated moulds are made). The details of this process are still secret, but it meant that Lilliput Lane could cut the time between the completion of the original

wax and the piece going into production from around three months to an average of four to five weeks. They were also able to make six moulds in the time it used to take to make one, and the use of different, highly complex materials meant that every mould could be made to last four times as long. In another significant development, David Tate designed and patented an innovative packaging system that was much easier to use and was warmly welcomed by retailers.

By mid-1990, the overwhelming success and popularity of Lilliput Lane's cottages had thoroughly eclipsed a number of other projects with which the company had, in the previous three years, became involved. It was clear to the management that the way ahead lay in devoting their attention entirely to the cottages, to the exclusion of their other concerns like the 'Land of Legend' and Albany Bone China of Stoke. A major restructuring of the company took place, leaving Lilliput Lane leaner and fitter as a leading company for the nineties. Chairman William Dodd became owner of 'Land of Legend', now independent of Lilliput Lane, and his place as Chairman and Managing Director was taken by John Russell, a Yorkshireman with a strong financial and management background. After a period of unexpected and prolific growth, with all its excitements and attendant strains, a new era was beginning at Lilliput Lane, characterised by single-minded dedication to consistent development and improvement of their cottages and of their service to collectors.

LILLIPUT LANE TODAY

Today finds the company in a strong position, enjoying both a well-deserved and stoutly defended reputation for top quality and an international sphere of influence that is constantly extending. Lilliput Lane cottages are keenly collected but they are all still made in Cumbria, and it is here that the secrets of their success may be discovered, as a closer look at the workings of the company today will reveal.

The most significant factor in the company's success has, of course, been the cottages themselves. From the original fourteen models, there are now over 169 in production with new ideas being generated all the time. Though Lilliput Lane's cottages may have become far more complex and ambitious over the years, the principles on which they rest remain the same as ever. These principles — that the integrity of design and quality of execution of the cottages are paramount — are allied to the desire to offer the best value for money to collectors. Adherence to these standards is apparent in every aspect of day-to-day work at Lilliput Lane, from the extensive research that goes into every new piece to ensure its authenticity, to the precision mould-making, allowing every detail to be captured, and the intense scrutiny to which every piece is subjected before it is allowed out of the workshops. In every department, these standards are applied in the tireless efforts to maintain and improve quality while keeping costs down.

But without the work force, nothing would be possible. Having started with just seven, nine years later the company employs around 700 people. One of the remarkable features of Lilliput Lane is the youth of these people, whose average age is only twenty-seven, with many of the junior managers under twenty-six. 'There's a massive energy in youth,' says David Tate, 'and it is not constrained by fixed ideas and preconceptions, so anything is possible. Change and innovation are always welcomed.' Keen to help everyone fulfil their true potential, Lilliput Lane strongly encourages youthful enthusiasm, harnessing it to the benefit of individuals and the company alike.

The majority of the work force was employed at the company's four Cumbrian sites, Penrith, Cockermouth, Workington

Below, the Tate family at Buckingham palace in 1988, for the induction of David as a Member of the British Empire (MBE). Queen Elizabeth II presided over the ceremony.

The Queen's Award for Export, highly prized among British companies.

larger than the original tiny unit, and extends to include nearly all the old farm buildings, from the stable block to the former chicken sheds and many outer houses. Though these have all been fully modernised to make them suitable for current use, this has been achieved with sensitivity to their origins, using bare wood and white paint to retain a functional and honest simplicity. Here as ever, all the research and development takes place, though David Tate's team of twenty has now spread into a range of workshops and studios clustered around the yard. This is the nerve-centre for innovation, where new ideas take their first tortuous steps from initial drawings towards reality, via countless rigorous tests, and new materials are investigated and put through their paces to see what improvements they may offer.

This constant questing to better the product is a characteristic of Lilliput Lane that has been central to its success. At Lilliput Lane, complacency has no place. Problems are seen as opportunities, and the management is never afraid to make a radical change if it thinks it is for the best. Throughout its history, well-established production systems have been regularly overhauled and even scrapped altogether whenever a new development or discovery promises improvement. The last year bears witness to this, with a list of major

and Cleator Moor. Production is divided amongst these sites according to their particular facilities, and the management, ever intent on making the best use of its resources, constantly reviews and adjusts this allocation. With such high demand and such stringent standards, it is essential that maximum efficiency is maintained, with every department and individual working to full capacity. The chain of production depends on this, for each department can only work as fast as the previous one produces — the painters have nothing to paint if the casters are behind.

The original site at Skirsgill, Penrith, now occupies an area many times

Blaise Hamlet, now reproduced in miniature as a Lilliput Lane collection, was designed by the famous 19th-century architect John Nash after the vernacular styles of the Cotswolds.

developments that embraces everything from tool-making to the revolutionary new system of packing. Many of the technical advances push the boundaries of model-making and loosen the constraints of the production process, allowing more and more complex shapes to be cast. This makes the artists free to sculpt ever finer and more detailed pieces. As David Tate remarks, 'We will not accept any limitations imposed on the sculptors by the needs of the mould-makers. If the sculptors have a limitation, it is our job to find a way to remove it.'

All new models are introduced into pre-production at Penrith first, so that any initial technical problems can be quickly sorted out by the Research and Development team on site. Some of the largest and most complex models take many months to bring to perfection, and even then production often stays at Penrith to ensure smooth running. Most of the models are, however, allocated to the other sites. Casting takes place either at Penrith or at Workington, where sophisticated equip-

ment has substantially improved casting times. Once the models are dry and ready for painting and finishing, they may be sent to any of the sites, where highly trained teams of painters bring them to life through the application of a carefully chosen palette of over fifty colours.

Though they are removed from each other by several miles, the sites are closely co-ordinated in their work through the supervision of the Production Director. It is his job to make sure that all the sites are not only working to maximum efficiency but are also fulfilling the demand from the marketplace. According to the feedback gleaned from the sales department about which pieces are, and will be, in demand, the efforts of each site are directed into making the appropriate pieces to fulfil the orders. Every day, early in the morning, the Lilliput Lane lorry loads up with raw materials at the bulk warehouse at Gil-willy near Penrith. It then sets off on its daily round, delivering raw materials to each site, and bringing back the finished models so that they can be despatched to the retailers from the warehouse.

Meanwhile, the Lilliput Lane sales team goes out on the road, meeting some of their 1,500 chosen retailers in this country. They listen to their requirements, picking up valuable information about which cottages are currently popular and what reactions they have experienced from their customers. They tell them of new products in the pipeline, and are keen to support the retailers and give them swift, effective service. Sometimes they arrange for a special visit by one of the painters from Lilliput Lane, who can demonstrate to the customers the care and skill involved in painting each piece. Such promotional visits are enormously popular, as one retailer recalls. 'We were completely unprepared for the success of our first promotion,' says Mrs Isherwood of Joseph Bailey (Bolton) Ltd. 'The shop was bursting and people were spilling out onto the pavement, bartering and swapping cottages amongst themselves as they waited to get in. Many of them just ordered all the new pieces straight off, without even seeing them. Lilliput Lane collectors are certainly something else. . . .'

A key factor in the continuing success of Lilliput Lane is close co-ordination between the different departments, exemplified in the spirit of teamwork that is apparent in every area. Everybody's contribution is valued, and there are regular meetings that allow representatives of every department concerned to voice their opinions on the decisions of the day. These cover all aspects of the business, from the finer points of a new model, still only at the sculpting stage, to the content of the newly designed catalogue, or the plans for the next collectors' jamboree. These meetings are informal, and they offer a forum for free debate and the airing of many diverse views that not only provides an important sounding board for the company but also keeps everyone in touch with developments.

Close control of production is essential to success, and this has never been more stringently monitored than it is now. With the conflicting exigencies of high quality and reasonable cost, there is no room for wastage, and much effort is directed towards improvements that will allow reject rates to be kept down. Because it believes in giving its collectors only the best, no rejects are ever allowed onto the market in any form (they are all assiduously smashed into a skip before dumping), so they do represent lost time and money.

Keeping reject rates down depends on a number of technical factors, but it has not escaped the management that staff

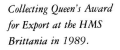

Collecting Queen's Award for Export at the HMS Brittania in 1989.

● National award winners
PM TOASTS BOOM FIRM'S SUCCESS

PENRITH boom company Lilliput Lane have won a prestigious award for their in-house training program.

The company — who have grown from seven to over 700 employees in seven years — are one of only eighty in the country to have been honoured with the national training award.

The win came in Lilliput Lane's first entry into the three-year-old contest, and competition came from over 1,300 other top companies across the country.

Prime Minister Mrs. Margaret Thatcher sent a personal letter of congratulation to the firm's Skirsgill headquarters.

She said: "Your success in winning an award is a clear demonstration of your commitment to sound investment in training.

"Your success reflects the hard work and effort of management and employees alike. It is more important than ever that others in industry and commerce in the United Kingdom should learn from your example," added Mrs. Thatcher.

The award to Lilliput Lane was announced at a special ceremony at the Queen Elizabeth II Conference Centre, London, last Thursday. It was attended by group personnel manager Dawn Wylie

NATIONAL TRAINING AWARD MCMLXXXIX

Among the guests were the Secretary of State for Employment, Mr. Norman Fowler, and leading television and media figures. The ceremony was introduced by newscaster Moira Stewart.

"It is good recognition for the staff. I think they can really feel proud that the skills they have developed and the training program we have has justified such an award. It is a result of their skills really," said Dawn Wylie.

"There is very little mechanisation. We are very labour intensive and, therefore, our success depends on the skills of the workforce," she added.

SUCCESS

Lilliput Lane's road to success in the awards scheme began in May with the official entry in the category for companies which have created their own in-house training programs.

Judges made their own inspection and evaluation in Summer, resulting in a recommendation to the North West regional judging panel to award a certificate of commendation and, eventually, leading to top national honours.

Lilliput Lane's training scheme has been continually improved throughout the past seven years.

"We started training from the bare essentials and moved on from there. Painters, for example, were trained on a one-to-one basis until they developed the full skills required," said Dawn.

Despite the growth of the company, the one-to-one training method continues, and each employee undergoes a 26-week training program.

Each of the 750 workers on Lilliput Lane's four Cumbrian sites has taken part in in-house training schemes, including management, whose training was devised with the help of external consultants.

Instead of taking on sales agents, Lilliput Lane opted to create their own sales department.

SKILLS

Training has been designed to develop workers' skills to the full and company policy is to promote from within the workforce where possible.

From an initial £123,000 in 1983, turn-over has risen to a current £7.5 million and the company have been named for two years' running by the CBI as one of the top five outstanding young companies.

Another major success came in 1987 when the company won a Queen's Award for Export.

satisfaction and involvement is also one of them. People who are happy in their work and feel it is valued do their job more carefully and successfully. This fact was borne out at Lilliput Lane early on in its history when the company experimented with a 'conveyor belt' system of painting — each person painting just one colour on each cottage before passing it on to another painter for the next colour. It was a disaster. The painters derived none of the satisfaction they had done from painting one piece completely, painting times for each piece was doubled and quality went down. Having learnt a valuable lesson, they quickly reverted to the original system.

THE COLLECTORS

Despite its expanded size, Lilliput Lane still generates an informal family atmosphere. A sense of belonging is not confined only to the employees, but is extended by the company to the collectors too, through close involvement with the Collectors' Club. The collectors are highly regarded by the company, and they are a significant influence on the company today. Every opportunity is taken to canvass their views of its products and to respond to their wishes.

The Lilliput Lane Collectors' Club now boasts over 30,000 members worldwide, with branches in America, Canada, Australia, and New Zealand. Back at Penrith, the club is managed by an enthusiastic team, who are kept busy answering hundreds of letters, enquiries and phone calls everyday (2,000 enquiries about membership are received every month). They know many of the collectors personally and enjoy keeping in touch with their regular correspondents. Members of the Collectors' Club receive a full-colour quarterly magazine, *Gulliver's World*, which gives them all the news about the company and offers them previews of new pieces that have yet to find their way into the shops. Every year they get a special free gift (1991 sees a cottage as the members' gift for the first time), not available to non-members. Lilliput Lane also regularly offers its collectors special pieces, exclusive to the membership (recent Collectors' Club Specials have included Lavender Cottage in 1989, Bridle Way in 1990 and Gardeners Cottage in 1991). They are also offered priority in Limited Editions, a significant privilege in view of the speed with which such pieces sell out.

Having had only the most limited ability to show collectors round the workshops, yet wanting to involve them further, Lilliput Lane has established an annual Collectors' Fair. Highly successful and popular events were held at Greystoke Castle in 1989, and Shugborough in 1990, the latter attracting an astonishing 10,000 visitors who turned out to meet Lilliput Lane. These were family events with entertainments for children as well as slide shows, talks, demonstrations and tours round the house. At Shugborough old country traditions were represented by local Morris dancers and displays by a Master Thatcher. There were countless opportunities to understand the many skills that go into every Lilliput Lane piece. Visitors were even given the chance to paint their own cottage, a salutary experience that revealed to them just how complex a task it is. The 1991 event was held at Ragley Hall in Warwickshire.

The passion that Lilliput evokes in collectors is now widely recognised, and many collectors describe themselves as 'enjoying an addiction'. Collector Karen Scrivener of Harlow speaks for many when she describes the appeal of Lilliput Lane cottages to her. 'They represent a miniature world of fantasy,' she says, 'and they have such a magical charm that I want to be part of it. I lose myself in them, and they let me dream about opening the door and walking in, being at home in the thatched cottage myself. And each one brings with it a pleasant memory of how I found it — a day in the country, or perhaps a long but successful search via one of the overseas friends I've made through collecting Lilliput Lane. With so many awful things in the world today, it is wonderful to find something so enjoyable.'

Lilliput Lane has such a broad appeal that it is impossible to profile a typical collector. Their enthusiasm shows itself in many ways — some cross continents to find rare pieces; others make a hobby of trying to track down and visit the original inspiration for each cottage, and yet others just enjoy the fun and write poems about it. One collecting couple even sold a horse to finance the conversion of their garage into a showroom for their Lilliput Lane collection. There are those who chronicle Lilliput Lane with an almost academic intensity, like Henry Grainger of Tyne and Wear. He has not only collected every piece ever made by Lilliput (and in every version), but he has made a serious study of the dates of every introduction, reworking and deletion, keeping this information in numerous, carefully compiled, volumes.

The Collectors' Club also has some very young members — their youngest ever was registered even before he was born. Many others save all their pocket money to buy Lilliput Lane cottages, sometimes with spectacular results. Ben Lee started his collection four years ago at the age of eleven, buying Bridge House. 'I am fascinated by architecture,' he says, 'and these pieces are just so nice and English.' With money earned on his paper round, and contributions from birthdays and Christmas, he has saved enough to buy even St Peter's Cove. Though his hi-fi-buying friends think he is crazy, he is confident that time will show his investment to be the better one.

The company maintains a close relationship with its chosen retailers, giving them the best possible service and support. And the retailers are keen to stock such a successful and popular product. One of the major retailers, Mrs Viv Marston at the Eden Craft Gallery in Penrith, expresses the enthusiasm of many when she says that 'Nothing has yet rivalled the quality of Lilliput Lane. Since the early days, it has taken off in an amazing way, and we now sell cottages to visitors from all over the world.'

Many of the retailers have also started to respond to the demand for pieces that are scarce or no longer available, making for a healthy secondary market, and proving the current investment value of Lilliput Lane. This is further enhanced by the company's policy of regularly retiring pieces after a certain period irrespective of any continuing demand. 'We care about the collectors,' says David Tate, 'and we want to maintain the collectability of our cottages by controlling the numbers rather than just exploiting them.'

Current Chairman and Managing Director, John Russell.

LILLIPUT LANE — INTO THE NINETIES

Despite a secure present and a bright future, there remains no room for complacency at Lilliput Lane. 'We want to build on what we have here already,' says Chairman John Russell. 'We must keep in touch with the traditions of this business, the integrity and quality for which we have become known, while pushing forward the bounds of creativity and amazing people at what we can produce.' With the continuing rate of technical development, there is no doubt that the tradition of improving quality will be maintained, with all the excitement it implies for new products. The standards set by David Tate will also assure the future integrity of any new Lilliput Lane product, whatever it is and wherever it is from.

Controlled development is seen as the key to the future, and Lilliput Lane is steadily increasing its influence, not only in this country but around the world. Gift Link has already achieved a sound basis in the United States, with Lilliput Lane's cottages and their America Landmarks collection becoming increasingly popular. Collectors can now also buy Lilliput Lane in Canada, Australia, New Zealand, South-East Asia and Japan, and new distributors are being found all the time to widen the global network. It is hoped that *Gulliver's World* will one day carry a newsletter in a number of languages for the benefit of overseas collectors.

Meanwhile nearer to home, the 1992 date for the freeing of trade within Europe is not forgotten, and Lilliput Lane continues to explore the possibilities of Europe. With an established German Collection already to its credit, the French Collection was launched in the autumn of 1990, and a new Dutch Collection reached completion in the spring of 1991. Hitherto such national collections have been available only in their respective countries, but Lilliput Lane is going truly European, and making them available in Britain too.

The collectors are uppermost in mind as Lilliput Lane goes forward into the nineties. 'Our collectors are special people,' says John Russell, 'and we should always aim to do more for them.' Bearing this in mind, in acknowledgement of their collectors' great interest in its past, Lilliput Lane is opening a Collectors' Centre at Penrith, which will comprise a museum of all its pieces. Here collectors will be welcomed, and they can find out just what the rare early pieces look like, as well as view the entire contemporary range.

Lilliput Lane remains a company that is dedicated to the pleasure, happiness and *joie de vivre* that its products offer those that buy them. In order to bring more surprises and more fun to its collectors, it strives constantly to find new, exciting ways of improving what it does. The spirit of Lilliput Lane's quest for a better product is best captured by David Tate. 'When I'm asked which is the best piece Lilliput Lane has ever done, I say, "We haven't done it yet — we're working on it!" '

Cottages from Britai

The Cot

urope & America

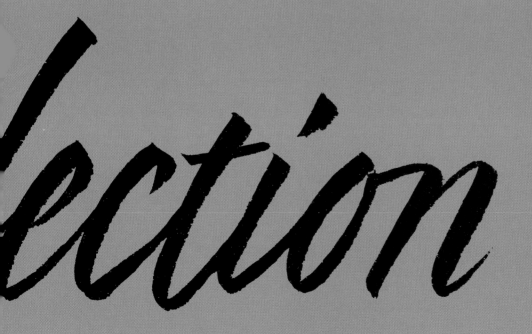

Those who have travelled in Great Britain will know how rich it is in the heritage of the past and what charm this lends it, both in town and country. There are the great stately homes, justly famous for the splendours of their architecture. But to David Tate, the real magic of the English heritage lies not in grandeur, but in the rich variety of small, unpretentious dwellings that he has observed in his travels around the country. Tucked away in tiny

villages, down farm tracks and between the hedgerows he has found buildings so perfectly at one with their surroundings that they seem to have grown there, their very roofs, whether undulating thatch or honest slate, forming an integral part of the landscape. They are timeless, appearing unmoved by the passing of the years, and they offer a tangible link with an ever more distant past. Enchanted by them, David Tate was inspired to share this magical heritage with others, capturing it in miniature at Lilliput Lane.

The cottages that inspire David's passion are described as vernacular. This term is applied to the buildings made by local people for their own purposes, using materials easily available to them in their neighborhood. The methods they used and the appearance of the buildings they created depended on local tradition and materials, rather than fashionable designs and state-of-the-art techniques. The latter were the province of the wealthy, who could afford to follow fashion and to transport expensive building materials to their chosen site. Their buildings, commonly referred to as examples of 'polite' architecture, tend to have far less to do with locality than with contemporary styles and published designs.

Though examples of building in the local tradition exist from the 15th to the 19th centuries, the hey-day of vernacular architecture in Britain was the 16th and 17th centuries. From earlier than this, the great majority of small, medieval, vernacular homes have long since disappeared, their frail, one-roomed structure having only been expected to last perhaps one generation before rebuilding. These dwellings would have been constructed by those who occupied them, without the benefit of skilled craftsmanship; the only concern was to achieve some sort of shelter for the few hours that they were not at work in the fields.

Great changes in society were wrought by the plague of 1348, which is estimated to have reduced the population by a third. With the work force so radically cut back, many landowners took up sheep farming, since it required less labour than arable farming. Over the following centuries, great wealth was generated through the wool trade and found expression in building. It was not only the well-to-do landowners who were able to build but also some of the humbler people who benefitted from the break-up of the feudal system, establishing their freedom to work profitably, whether on a small holding or at their chosen trade.

During the reign of Queen Elizabeth I (1558–1603), the population rose rapidly, and the increased demand for housing, combined with the spread of wealth, led to a golden age of building. One-roomed medieval cottages were gradually superseded by cottages with two rooms, and often an upper storey too. Since communications were poor, and travel and transport remained expensive luxuries, people continued to use the building materials they found around them. England was extensively forested in those days, so timber was plentiful. Many of the timber-framed cottages with which we are familiar today date from this period and from the first half of the 17th century.

It is important to realise that many of the buildings of this period, which we refer to today as cottages, were originally occupied not by labourers and peasants, but by farmers, tradesmen and other citizens by no means at the bottom of the social scale. The land that went with their cottage gave them a living, and it could be supplemented by a cottage industry like spinning or weaving. By the early 18th century, many had established a reasonable standard of living, with sufficient food (mostly grown themselves) and enough fuel for a good fire.

By contrast, the homes of the poor made little progress from medieval times right through the 18th century. They constructed and occupied the most makeshift of hovels, usually not even weatherproof, and their lot remained unutterably dismal even as others enjoyed the 18th century's 'Age of Elegance'. Homelessness was a real threat, since even the erection of such meagre shelters was a matter of debate and dispute within every parish. Traditionally, if a man could put up a roof over his head without being caught and kindle a fire to demonstrate his residence, he could stay there, and after a mere sixty years he would be granted a freehold.

The death knell of true vernacular building was sounded by the Industrial Revolution of the late 18th and early 19th centuries. The countryside depopulated as people flocked to the towns in search of work, and local building traditions waned. The vernacular customs were further eroded by the development of roads and railways, which gave ready access to non-local, mass-produced building materials, though in remote areas, local traditions lasted longer. Ironically, as industrialisation was spelling the end of the vernacular, its beneficiaries began to become sentimental about rural architecture. They copied the vernacular styles, creating 'picturesque' dwellings that echoed a rural idyll from a time gone by. Blaise Hamlet is an example of such 'picturesque' architecture, built by John Nash in 1810–11.

As the 19th century progressed, the nostalgic yearning for a lost rural idyll grew, fuelled by the 'Romantic' movement which idealised nature. Escape from the dirt and smog of urban life was highly desirable, and those who could afford them acquired country cottages as second homes. Cottages began to be seen not as the despised dwellings of the poor, but as romantic, rustic retreats for the well-to-do, an attitude still current today in our concept of the 'dream cottage'. This infatuation with the beauties of the countryside and the 'simple life' developed to fever pitch in Victorian times, finding expression in the arts as well. Those who could not afford their own cottage retreat might buy one of the many pretty pottery and porcelain model cottages made in the first half of the 19th century. Some of these served a useful purpose as pastille burners, reminding one of the rustic dream while disguising the smell of urban smog with fragrant incense. Cottages were also a favourite subject for painters, and many examples of their work exist today, depicting perfect thatched cottages with abundant gardens bursting with delphiniums and roses.

Cottages that have survived the passing centuries and exist today were, by definition, soundly built. The men who built them knew their materials and handled them well, employing tried and trusted techniques, passed down from father to son over generations. Whether this was the manipulation and joining of timbers to create a sound frame, the careful selection and laying of local stones to build a wall, or the well-tried compressing of mud and straw into cob, it is the combination of

these traditional techniques with the local materials that gives the cottages we admire today their special charm. Because the materials used are local, they have a natural affinity with the immediate environment and blend perfectly with their surroundings.

So clearly do the truly vernacular cottages of England reflect their own environment that the practised eye can read the clues they offer in their appearance, and establish their regional identity. The angle of the thatch, the colour of the slate, the decorative pargeting of a wall, all these characteristics together make up, David Tate believes, a hidden map of the countryside, which can offer any lost traveller all the indication he needs as to his location. Lilliput Lane cottages capture this 'hidden map' perfectly in miniature, as the following pages show.

*T*he South-east of England, from the windswept fens of East Anglia down south to Kent, the lush 'Garden of England', and across westwards as far as the Isle of Wight, is an area blessed with a wide range of naturally occuring building materials that makes for rich and varied vernacular traditions. Many existing cottages date back to the 15th and 16th centuries when oak grew freely in England; indeed, it has been said to have grown

'like a weed' in Sussex. Despite the anxieties of the Elizabethans who feared an oak shortage because of their extensive felling (for naval and fuel purposes), timber-framing continued to be widely employed. Oak was not seasoned before use, which explains the characteristic and endearing distortions seen today on old timber-framed buildings.

In East Anglia, the eye is easily deceived at first glance, since timber-framing is often concealed beneath a covering of plaster, applied for the purposes of weather-proofing. Far from lacking the decorative appeal of exposed timber buildings, many of these cottages are adorned with ornamental pargetting. This traditional skill involved the application of decorative patterns to the plaster while still soft, using sticks and combs. Many notable examples of this 16th- and 17-century craft may be seen in the villages of Suffolk and Essex.

Also typical of East Anglian cottages are the colour washes applied to the plaster. In Suffolk, pink was especially popular, and there is a theory that Suffolk Pink came from pigs' blood, or sloe juice. What is delightful and characteristic about colour washes is their lack of uniformity, and the multitude of gently blending tones that can be seen looking up a village street.

Moving westwards into Hertfordshire, the plaster-clad cottages give way to the exposed timbers more typical of the Midlands. Further south, a mixture of timber-framed buildings is seen, some with timbers exposed to show their construction, and some concealed. The southern counties of Kent, Surrey and Sussex have such cottages, and the Sussex Weald is home to one of the most well-known types, the Wealden house. This has an attractive 'jettied' upper storey, projecting beyond the lower walls.

Though widely used elsewhere also, thatch for roofing is a particular characteristic of East Anglia, and there are more thatched cottages in Suffolk than in any other county. This is explained by the proximity of the extensive reed beds of the Norfolk Broads, reed making the best thatching material. A good reed thatch can last sixty years. The thatched roofs of the eastern counties are typically steeply pitched and often rise slightly at either end of the ridge. Alternatives to thatch included pantiles (curved roofing tiles), imported from the Netherlands from the late 17th century and often used in eastern counties to replace thatch. Further south, where the quality of local clay meant that good hand-made tiles were readily available, these were a common choice for roofing. The tiled roofs of Kent, Surrey

and East Sussex owe their character to the beauty and variety of local clay.

Bricks made from local earth also find their way into some of the cottages of the South-east. In some cottages they are laid in decorative patterns between the timbers as in-filling, known as 'brick-nogging', in place of the earlier wattle and daub. Elsewhere, particularly where timber was in short supply, for example the open Fen Lands and in north Norfolk, brick forms a primary building material. It is often used to form quoins (corner-stones of walls and windows) and is combined with rough local flint in-fill. Early brick has a local character, variety and irregularity that clearly distinguished it from its later uniform, mass-produced descendant, which took over around 1800.

Further protection from the weather was sometimes sought, and in Suffolk and Essex, weather-boarding is seen, with overlapping planks applied to the upper sections of the walls. Further south, clay tiles were hung on the walls for the same purposes. Both of these techniques were often applied many years later, and along with other later additions often disguise old timber-framed structures.

Sussex Mill I

Sussex Mill II

April Cottage II   *April Cottage I*

Oak Lodge II   *Oak Lodge I*

Coach House

Coopers

Old Shop at Bignor

John Barleycorn Cottage

Flower Sellers

Hopcroft Cottage

The King's Arms

Anne of Cleves

54

Stone Cottage

Acorn Cottage I

Acorn Cottage II   *Honeysuckle Cottage*

56

Kentish Oast House   *Millers*

Toll House

Clare Cottage

Swift Hollow

Bay View

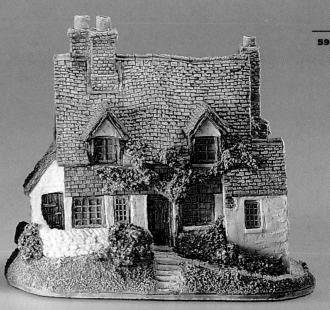

Pargetters Retreat

Brockbank

Mrs. Pinkerton's Post Office

Wight Cottage

Chine Cot 1   *Chine Cot II*   *Cherry Cottage*

The Rising Sun

Daisy Cottage

Bramble Cottage

Strawberry Cottage

Greensted Church

Primrose Hill

Ash Nook   *The Old Curiosity Shop*

66

The Gables

Tanglewood Lodge

The Swan Inn   *The Crown*

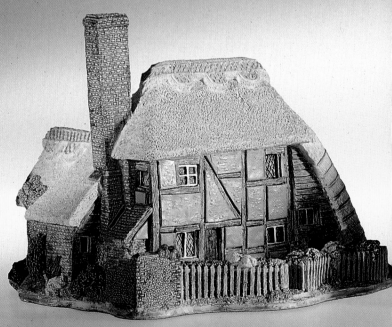

Three Feathers

Saxon Cottage

Thatcher's Rest

Wealden House

St. Peter's Cove

The south-western peninsula of England, jutting out into the Atlantic Ocean, has a character so much its own that from time to time in its history its people have sought independence from the rest of England. It is an area rich in folk-lore and legend that stretch back to pre-historic times. Dominated inland by acres of wild, rolling moorland, the furthest stretch of its craggy coast is scattered with tiny fishing villages clinging on in defiance of the

elements. The sea crashes on rugged, rocky headlands where wreckers used to lure ships to their doom. But this is a land of contrasts, and not far away the peaceful sandy coves and steep, tree-lined river estuaries where kingfishers dart has made this an area beloved of holiday-makers.

This was not a densely wooded area, so those who wished to build selected materials other than timber. Granite is the local stone, and makes an ideal building material. It is, however, extremely hard and therefore difficult to quarry, so local people would pick up loose granite from the moorlands for their own building purposes. Stones gathered in such a way varied in size enormously, and walls including stones of all shapes and sizes are a characteristic of the old granite cottages of the area. How the stones were placed was, however, carefully thought out, with the largest making a sound footing for the

71

wall, and the smallest filling in gaps further up. To make such walls proof against the frequent westerly gales, they would be packed with earth, pebbles and mortar, and finally coated with colour-washed plaster or perhaps faced with local slates. In Cornwall most of the roofs are of local, dark grey slate, while in Devon they had a beautiful, richly textured slate.

Where stone was not readily available, the cottage builders used the earth itself as their building material. The lack of timber meant that they had no fuel to bake the earth into bricks, so they bonded it into a suitable texture by mixing it with straw, lime and water and treading it into a thick, fibrous pulp known in Devon as 'cob'. This was then laid on a sturdy stone foundation, in a layer some two feet high, and left to dry out and harden, before another layer was applied. The whole process could take several months, depending on the weather. In order to prevent the cob cracking as it dried out, the external corners of the buildings were rounded, giving the cob cottages of Devon their charming, cosy appearance. The final touch would be a coat of white limewash

for waterproofing (common in the north, Devon), or a colour wash (in the south).

Cob had the advantages of being cheap, and requiring no great craftsmanship to use, so that anybody could build his own home. Built into walls usually at least two feet thick, it was also an excellent insulator, making for a snug interior, as long as the exterior was well maintained against the weather. It was said that all a cob cottage needed was 'a good hat and a good pair of shoes', — a sound foundation and a weatherproof roof. Since it has no inbuilt framework, a cob cottage had to have a lightweight roof that would also protect the walls by throwing rain well clear of them. Thatch was ideal for this purpose (straw rather than reed in this area), and its gentle undulating outlines rest perfectly with the cosy curves of the many cob cottages of the South-west.

Convent in the Woods

Periwinkle Cottage

The Smallest Inn

Ostlers Keep

The Royal Oak

Butterwick

The Briary

Spring Bank

Clover Cottage

Fishermans Cottage

Moonlight Cove

Woodcutters   *The Old Post Office*

Otter Reach

Watermill

Titmouse Cottage

Tintagel

This area, the heartland of England, has always been rich in raw materials and has derived lasting fame and fortune from them. Naturally occurring coal and iron deposits made the northern towns the cradle of the Industrial Revolution, and potteries that remain famous today developed here in the 18th century. Further south in Warwickshire is the town of Stratford-upon-Avon, known throughout the world as the birthplace

of England's most famous son, the dramatist William Shakespeare. Westward are the counties bordering Wales, areas of great natural beauty, while bordering the Midlands to the south are the much-loved Cotswold hills, with the mellow stone villages.

The West Midlands was originally extensively forested, and being readily available, timber was widely used in building from early times well into the 18th century. Today the area is renowned for its numerous half-timbered buildings, often dubbed 'Magpie' houses because of the characteristic contrast between their blackened timbers and their whitewashed in-fill

of wattle and daub (twigs and clay). Wherever industrialisation has not swept them away, these houses are to be seen, and this area has a wider variety of timber buildings than any other in the country.

Two kinds of construction predominate amongst timber-framed buildings and both are abundant here. Cruck construction is the older, where pairs of curving timbers, joined at their apex and spaced with tie-beams from the basic structure supporting walls and roof. Often the crucks have been concealed by the cladding used to make the walls, but in the

West Midlands, where the walls were timber framed, these crucks can clearly be seen.

The second type of construction seen here is post-and-panel, which follows the same principles as cruck construction, but carries the roof load on a series of parallel frames, rather than joined pairs of curving timbers. This construction gives rise to the regular, square panelling seen on so many houses in this area, the panels being filled with wattle and daub, finished with plaster and typically whitewashed. As they became more generally available, local bricks might be used as a stronger in-fill on the ground floor, leaving the wattle and daub for the upper storey.

Another construction method led to the close placing of vertical timbers, creating long thin panels (a technique called close-studding) and where there was money to spare, all sorts of decorative wooden ornamentation was added to the panels. Examples of this elaborate technique are to be seen in the western counties of the Midlands and in East Anglia.

These timber-framed cottages were traditionally roofed with thatch, though many roofs in towns were later replaced with slate or tiles to reduce the considerable fire risk thatch represented.

There is another, quite distinct, strain of vernacular architecture that is characteristic of the southern and eastern border of the Midlands. Cotswold stone, a warm, creamy yellow limestone, occurs in a band that runs diagonally across England from Dorset in the south, up to Lincolnshire in the East Midlands and on to the Humber. With ready supplies of this good building stone, and money generated by the burgeoning wool trade, the village craftsmen of the Cotswolds developed techniques of working this stone that make their cottages so famous today. Cotswold cottages reflect a meticulous care and concern for architectural detailing that was rare in 17th-century village building. Typically, they have a high dormer, allowing light into the upper storey. Their roofs are of local limestone tiles. Cotswold architecture is echoed throughout the limestone belt, and those visiting places as far afield as Stamford in Lincolnshire will be put oddly in mind of the Cotswolds by the similarity of style and stone.

Paradise Lodge

Anne Hathaway's 1989

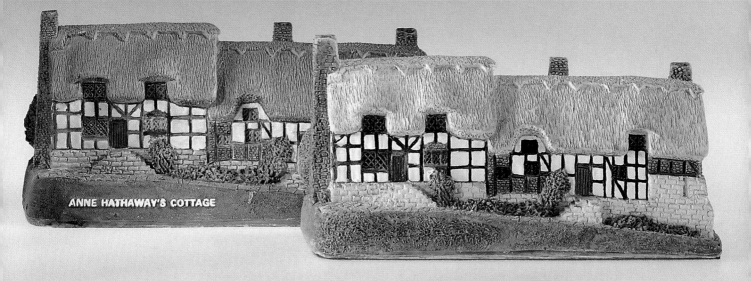

ANNE HATHAWAY'S COTTAGE

87

Anne Hathaway's I   *Anne Hathaway's II*

Moreton Manor

Drapers

St. Mary's Church

Tudor Court

Armada House

Four Seasons

Magpie Cottage

William Shakespeare's Birthplace

William Shakespeare's Birthplace 1989   *Beehive Cottage*

94

Bredon House   *St. Marks*

Pear Tree House   *Sulgrave Manor*

Summer Haze

Witham Delph

Tillers Green

Wellington Lodge

Lace Lane

Lapworth Lock

Farthing Lodge

Farriers

Buttercup Cottage

Robins Gate

Riverview

Fiveways

Saddlers Inn

Cobblers Cottage

Tanners Cottage

In the North of England, the land rises up into the Pennines, and the scenery changes as the timbered Midland villages give way to rugged hills and valleys, lakes and moors. Here cottages have been built of hard-wearing local stone for centuries, the skills of their builders dedicated entirely to the creation of sound dwellings to brave the wind and weather. The solid, well-crafted cottages of the beautiful Lake District, only a few miles from Lilliput

Lane, have often been a source of inspiration to the sculptors.

The stone that was used for building in the North is of several different types. The most common stone in Yorkshire and the Pennines is a soft creamy yellow sandstone known as Yorkstone, which is dominant in the West Riding of Yorkshire and in the industrialised centres of the woollen trade. Running up from Nottinghamshire through Yorkshire to Durham is a band of limestone, which was much used in building the cottages of the Yorkshire Dales.

Another type of limestone, of a greyer hue, was used to the west in the Lake District of Cumbria. Sometimes this has been rendered and limewashed, but often it retains its natural appearance. Although such stone could be specially shaped or 'dressed' for the purposes of building neatly, this process was expensive, and it was much more common to use the stones as they came, placing them according to size.

This technique is called 'rough-faced random', and gives the walls their attractive irregular appearance. 'Best-faced random', where the showing face of the stones is squared, was used in larger houses.

Granite and slate were also used in Cumbria, the former sometimes built into walls without the benefit of mortar, and just whitewashed. Local Westmorland slate, typically green, blue or grey in colour, was split for use in roofing, and was sometimes used in larger pieces for walls. Roofing slates were graded by size, the larger ones being hung at the eaves and the smaller at the ridge, carefully overlapped to make a weatherproof roof. Over to the east, around York, there was access to imported pantiles for roofing, though heavy local flagstones were also used, requiring roofs to be of shallow pitch to take the weight.

Timber-framed buildings are uncommon, with the exception of some areas of Cheshire, and also the ancient city of York, which dates back to the 7th century. Here a narrow medieval street, The Shambles, is lined with quaint timber-framed buildings whose upper storeys nearly meet across the street.

Warwick Hall (front)

Warwick Hall (rear)

108

Lakeside House

Dale House

Burnside

Dale Farm

Bridge House 1991   *2nd Bridge House*   *1st Bridge House*

Dove Cottage No. 2

Dove Cottage No. 1

Tuck Shop   *Holly Cottage*

The Old School House

Miners

Castle Street

Troutbeck Farm   *Dale Head*

Brontë Parsonage

Dovetails

St. Lawrence Church

Village School

The Priest's House   *Chatsworth View*

Beacon Heights

Rydal View

Micklegate Antiques   *The Ship Inn*

Red Lion Inn

Runswick House

Victoria Cottage

Inglewood   *Keepers Lodge*

Helmere Cottage

Sawrey Gill

Holme Dyke   Stoneybeck

Secret Garden

SCOTLAND

A *land of rolling, heather-covered hills, rising to the craggy, snow-covered peaks of the Highlands and riven by sparkling lochs and peat-coloured burns, Scotland offers a rare, wild beauty. Its changeable, northern climate is well known, wind and rain being a commonplace, though*

always punctuated by clear days when the sun shines and the air is dazzling in its clarity. Through the centuries, the Scots have risen to the weather's challenge, building snug homes in defiance, and culling a living from their small crofts or farms, or from fishing.

Stone was the most widely used building material, especially locally occurring granite, and was employed not only in the austere, grey cities but also in the simple, rural cottages of outlying areas. Here, for better weatherproofing, the gaps between the stones were filled with peat to stop the draughts. In the remote 'blackhouses', windows were omitted altogether and appear today only as later additions.

Thatch of straw, or sometimes of heather, was widely employed for roofing, though it has often been replaced with slates. In the Northern Isles, the thatch was secured in position by weighted ropes. The poorest buildings were covered with squares of turf. Sandstone flags were used where available, and on the East Coast,

close links with the Low Countries are evident in the use of imported pantiles on 16th- and 17th-century buildings. French influence may also be seen in some grander buildings, due to Scotland's royal ties with France.

Scotland is steeped in legend and history, much of it embattled. Harsh times bonded people closely, and no ties were closer than those of blood that bound the members of each clan or family together. Fierce loyalties led to fierce conflicts, which in turn caused the building of the defensible strong houses or castles that still adorn the Scottish landscape. Their towering stone walls rise dauntingly out of the bedrock to deter attackers, and their magnificent, bleak austerity remains as impressive today as it was when they were built. Scotland's rich and diverse heritage is expressed in the dramatic contrasts of its dwellings, from cottages to castles, that have inspired Lilliput Lane's Scottish Collection.

Inverlochie Hame

The Croft

Hebridean Hame   *Fisherman's Bothy*

East Neuk

Preston Mill

Culloden Cottage

Carrick House

Eilean Donan Castle

Kinlochness   *Glenlochie Lodge*

Claypotts Castle   *Craigievar Castle*

Blair Atholl

Kirkbrae Cottage

Stockwell Tenement

John Knox House

Kenmore Cottage

Preston Mill (old)

7 St. Andrews Sq.

Burns' Cottage   *The Croft (no sheep)*

Cawdor Castle

WALES

Proud of its ancient heritage, with valleys echoing with song, and snow-capped peaks to the north, Wales still maintains a clear identity, with its own language and customs. Wales has long played a major part in shaping England's history, most significantly perhaps when the great Welsh dynasty of Tudors (Henry VII, VIII and Elizabeth I) ruled England from the late 15th century until 1603. Today, the male heir to the throne is invested as Prince of Wales, and Wales is thus a principality.

On its eastern border, Wales shares with that part of England the lush greenery and wooded lands that have given it a legacy of attractive, timber-framed houses. To the south of Wales are the great coalfields and mining towns, which in the dark days of the Industrial Revolution provided work for countless Welshmen, though often at a bitter price. Sandstone prevails down here, and it was used extensively for the simple housing of these mining towns.

Elsewhere in the country, hard rock and slate were the main building materials. In northern Wales, where the hills of Snowdonia rise up and the landscape becomes wild, cottages were built from the boulders that could be picked up, and their irregular, coarsely fashioned walls bear testament to this. Where the stone was dressed into more regular shapes, cottages of crisper, neater appearance are to be seen, their sharp angles and greater symmetry speaking of rather more sophistication than their rough-hewn counterparts. Roofs would be made of local slate. So prolific was this material that an industry grew up, sending the 'Welsh Blue' of Snowdonia to be employed on countless roofs, not only in Wales but all over.

Jutting out into the Atlantic's Gulf Stream, the south-west corner of Wales comprises fertile lands, where small villages of thatched and whitewashed cottages adorn the countryside. Famed for its beautiful Pembrokeshire coastline where nature still has a free hand, this area also has towns, such as Tenby, where an unexpected Flemish influence can be detected, dating back to the 12th century.

Wales has its share of grandeur as well as the enchanting simplicity of its cottages. Casting a long shadow back through history are many magnificent castles, including Caernarvon, Harlech, Cardiff and Chirk, bearing witness to a disturbed and troublesome past.

Bro Dawel   *Brecon Bach*   *Hermitage 1985*

Ugly House   *Hermitage 1990*

Tudor Merchant

IRELAND

The 'Emerald Isle' deserves its name, its wide rural expanses growing rich and verdant in the soft, showery climate. Its spectacular Atlantic coast contains arguably its most beautiful scenery, with mountain ranges and limpid lakes. Away to the east, the land becomes richer, and the living is

made easier in wide open pasturelands. Some have grown wealthy in Ireland, and there are marvellous great houses of gently decaying grandeur to be seen on rolling estate lands. But far more have struggled against poverty, persecution and famine in Ireland's troubled history. In the small cottages and rural dwellings of Ireland, integrity is to be found, and a true vernacular tradition.

The economy of Ireland over the centuries has been largely pastoral, and many followed a migratory existence, moving their herds from winter to summer pastures. Others farmed small crofts and lived in simple cottages built from local materials with techniques handed down from one generation to another. Though Ireland had been well wooded in medieval times, timber became scarce due to excessive felling for the purposes of war and industry. People used bog oak where it was available for timber, but they often had to build from other materials and typically used stone or clay. Clay was

bound with straw, like Devon cob, and once coated with limewash, this made a reasonably weatherproof house. The poorest dwellings, including those used as summer homes by herdsmen, were made of sods, piled up and then anchored down by flat stones and sometimes bound with clay. Roofs were typically a steeply pitched rough thatch of straw, marram grass or heather, lined with sods. In the areas more exposed to the weather, the thatch was secured with ropes.

The typical Irish house is long and narrow, one room leading to another, the width limited by the lack of long timbers. Often a house would be shared with the animals, one end becoming a byre. In some houses in Donegal, a lower floor was created for the animals by building out from the hillside. People would sleep in the room over the byre, enjoying the warmth from the animals.

St. Columba's School

Pat Cohan's Bar

Thoor Ballylee

O'Lacey's Store

Limerick House

St. Patrick's Church

Quiet Cottage

St. Kevin's Church

Donegal Cottage

Hegarty's Home

Magilligan's

Kilmore Quay

Ballykerne Croft

Kennedy Homestead

FRANCE

From the pretty villages of Normandy and Brittany in the north, to the Cote d'Azur on the sparkling blue Mediterranean in the south, from the wide open Atlantic beaches in the west, to the snowy Alps, France is a country of great natural beauty. While retaining the vitality of youth, the country has grown old gracefully, its magnificent palaces and chateaux perfectly complemented by the countless, unassuming dwellings of the ordinary people of the past

The range of materials available to the vernacular builder is as wide as the countryside is varied, and the evidence of this is to be seen in the way the style and character of dwellings changes from one region to another. In the south, where the river Rhone fans out to meet the Mediterranean, are the flat marshes of the Camargue, open lands haunted by wild white horses and flocks of birds. Here are simple, white-painted, two-roomed cottages with blue-painted wooden shutters around small windows to keep out the Mediterranean sun and, in turn, the wind. There dwellings are characteristically shaped with one rounded end to offer the least resistance to the high winds of the Mistral.

A little to the north is Provence, a particularly well-loved area of rural France, renowned for its famous wine. Here the yellow local stone walls are roofed with the half-round, terra-cotta tiles used in a manner unchanged since Roman times. The sun has bleached them to dappled shades of pale pink. A different sort of roof is characteristic of the luscious green, wooded Dordogne area, where there are many small farms. Animal shelters are made using a 'lauze' roof, where small limestone slabs are overlapped horizontally, and miraculously layered to form a closed roof with no internal support. Rather more homely is the farmhouse typical of the Perigord area, where the farmer and his family live above their animals, which shelter in the lower floor.

Away to the east, the border region of Alsace (long disputed and now proudly held by the French) still shows an unmistakable German influence in the superbly decorative, carved timber work in its little medieval towns. Timber-framing is seen again typically in northern France, in Normandy and Brittany. Here another delightful characteristic is the local thatch, often bound together with the roots of wild irises or lilies, which are planted in clay on the roof ridge. Granite is widely used in the simple cottages of Brittany, since the granite belt that runs through Britain from Scotland to Cornwall also extends south to here.

The rich tapestry of France's past is expressed not only in its many vernacular buildings but also in the magic of Parisian Montmartre and the grandeur of the famous chateaux of the Loire valley. Lilliput Lane's French Collection gives a sample of these numerous varied treasures, capturing France's many facets.

Le Mas du Vigneron
(The Vine Grower's House)

Le Manoir de Champfleuri
(*Pasture Lodge*)

Locmaria (Mary Cottage)

La Chaumière du Verger
(Orchard Cottage)

La Maselle de Nadaillac
(Nadaillac Shelter)

La Cabane du Gardian
(The Horse-Keepers Hut)

La Bergerie du Périgord
(Perigord Farmhouse)

La Porte Schoenenberg
(Shoenenberg Gatehouse)

L'Auberge d'Armorique
(Armorique Guest House)

Le Petit Montmartre
(Little Montmartre)

GERMANY

U*ntil only a hundred years ago, Germany was a multitude of distinct countries, including Saxony, Prussia and Bavaria, each with its own identity and traditions. Now together at last, Germany extends across a very large area of Europe, from the Baltic to the Alps, and despite its political*

unity it maintains a rich and diverse cultural heritage. This diversity is expressed in countless old cottages and towns, many dating back to the medieval period, showing Gothic influence and, later, baroque. Its handsome houses have a particular character of their own.

Germany has dense forests, and to these it owes its many fine timbered buildings, seen in town and country. The Germans have a word, *Fackwerke*, that conveys much more than just carpentry; it encompasses the fact that here timber is not merely a structural element but also a highly important decorative feature. The decoration of the wood with beautiful and elaborate carving is a source of particular pride in Germany.

The skill of the craftsmen who erected these timber-framed buildings was remarkable, for there is almost no limit to the variety they incorporated, from pillars to rounded turrets and curving gables. Above these structures rise steep, elegant roofs, which are often bravura displays of the

tiler's art. Some of the best examples are to be seen in the local town squares, where a fine old town hall may be flanked by a cheerful inn or two, and people can enjoy the striking of the hours on the town hall's carillon clock.

Away in the southern countryside are the little churches, with their characteristic onion-shaped spires, and along the road are pretty wayside shrines, used for centuries by the devout Catholics of the area. This part of the country has a different style of architecture, with quainter dwellings on a smaller scale, often adorned with flower-filled window boxes. Religious influence is evident again in the practice of painting religious subjects on the walls of some buildings.

Such a large, complex and varied country brims with potential for Lilliput Lane. Plans are afoot to extend and develop the German Collection, capturing more of the architectural gems of this colourful country for Lilliput Lane's collectors.

163

Haus im Rhineland
(House in the Rhineland)

164

Der Familienschrein
(The Family Chapel)

Jagdhütte
(Hunters Lodge)

Das Gebirgskirchlein
(*The Little Mountain Church*)

Die Kleine Bäckerei
(*The Small Bakery*)

Meersburger Weinstube
(Meersburg Wine Bar)

Moselhaus
(Moselle House)

167

Das Rathaus
(The Town Hall)

Nürnberger Bürgerhaus
(Nuremberg House)

Schwarzwaldhaus
(Black Forest House)

THE NETHERLANDS

With the majority of its land below sea-level, the Dutch people have long been used to managing water, whether by building dykes to keep the sea out or creating canals for transport. Water may threaten to engulf them, but it is also water-borne trade that made them one of the greatest trading nations

of the 17th century, with mastery of the seas and influence extending to far-off colonies. Unlike English domestic architecture, where the native tradition can most clearly be seen in the countryside, in Holland it was amongst the bustle of the towns that an individual, national style developed.

Along the canals that form main thoroughfares in Dutch towns, packed closely together are the picturesque houses of the merchants, appearing to jostle each other for space. They appear to stand end-on to the waterfront, their narrow elevations tapering to a gable of characteristic steepness. A number of different types of gable can be distinguished, amongst the best known being the stepped or stair gable, the gently curving clock gable, the neck gable (with vertical sides often supported by sculptured ornament) and the more severe, triangular, spout gable. The houses are much narrower than they are deep, and the ground floor rooms are exceptionally tall, the

room height steadily reducing floor by floor towards the sloping roof space. Light might be let into the roof space by a dormer, often a decorative feature in itself, with painted shutters and a little steep roof of its own.

Brick was the predominant building material for these houses, though stone and timber were occasionally used where available. But the bricks were by no means dull, varying in colour from rose to dark purple, and yellow to salmon pink. Full use was made of these different colours, and highly decorative effects were created through the contrasts. Town roofs were invariably of pantiles, which blend perfectly with the brickwork.

The true magic of Dutch architecture can only be appreciated by looking collectively, not at one house alone, but all along the waterfront, enjoying the harmonious eccentricities of their fantastic gables, pretty dormers and slender spires, each contrasting with the next.

De Wolhandelaar
(The Wool Merchant)

De Zijdewever
(The Silk Weaver)

De Pepermolen
(The Pepper Mill)

De Diamantair
(The Diamond Merchant)

Rozengracht
(Rose Canal)

Rembrandt van Rijn
(Rembrandt's House)

Begijnhof
(The Almshouse)

De Branderij
(The Distillery)

Aan de Amstel
(On The Amstel)

Bloemenmarkt
(The Flower Market)

Threw history of the United States is the colourful tale of brave pioneering spirits searching for freedom in what they called the New World. From England, Spain and France they came, from the Low Countries, Sweden and later central Europe, all seeking wealth, liberty or just a new future. With them they brought little, save their own skills, and from the land they found, they made their homes, pushing over westward into the heartland of America.

The vestiges of the old rural architecture of America that remain today represent the adaptation of imported European styles to the local climate and materials, and the evolution of a separate vernacular tradition. This is characterised by the extensive and skilful use of timber, a material available in abundance. It is seen particularly in the ubiquitous hewn-log construction of aging barns in the agricultural heartlands of America. Timber was also widely used in the 'clapboard' houses of New England, where wooden facings were found to be more practical than the English traditional wattle and daub.

The vast size of America has made travel a major part of its history, from the early pioneer days when men journeyed on foot, mule or wagon, to the coming of the railways and today's great interstate highways. Buildings associated with travel, like the railroad stations and the bridges, have a special romance to them, and even the old roadside barns have not escaped the impact of this itinerant heritage, decoratively daubed as they are with advertising slogans intended to catch the eye of travellers.

People settled where they could secure their livelihood, whether this was growing corn, tobacco or, in the Deep South, cotton. They built barns and farm buildings, a home for themselves and, to ensure their spiritual welfare, a church, which became the centre of the community. Most of these settlements have long been overtaken by new development. The houses have gone; the remaining barns are threatened, and the few tiny, early churches are empty.

The speed of progress in the United States has always been breathtaking, a mark of the enterprising nature of its complex population. Only fifty years separated the simple homesteaders, making a meagre living by laboriously tilling the land, from the arrival of mechanised farming and the great grain factories. In the vanguard of this development, much was swept away, and today there are few vestiges of the past to remind us of America's brave, early days. This vanishing past is recalled in Lilliput Lane's American Landmarks collection — from railroad station to chapel, cotton mill to country barns — sculpted by leading American artist Ray Day.

Adobe Church

Grist Mill   *Log Cabin*

Adobe Village
(with crosses & ladders)

Adobe Village
(without crosses & ladders)

Cape Cod Cottage

General Store 1

General Store II

Wallace Station

Midwest Barn

Lighthouse

Country Church

San Francisco House

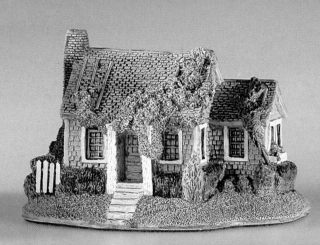

Roadside Coolers

Rambling Rose

Sign of the Times   School Days   Great Point Light

Victoriana

Country Church

Falls Mill

Pepsi Cola Barn

Countryside Barn

Hometown Depot

Covered Memories

Pioneer Barn   Mail Pouch Barn

Riverside Chapel

Fire House 1

Blaise Hamlet was the work of three men of exceptional talents. Humphrey Repton, the first landscape gardener, John Nash, the Prince Regent's architect and George Repton, assistant to Nash and son of Humphrey. It was here that their talents met when John Scandrett Hartford

commissioned Humphrey Repton to design a romantic and picturesque environment for his new mansion just outside Bristol. Nash provided the jewel in the crown of this ambitious project in 1810 with his designs for the cottages at Blaise Hamlet, inspired by the vernacular architecture of the Cotwolds.

The properties now belong to the National Trust and are considered to be the best example of their type in the country.

Lilliput Lane's collection consists of nine models, the first three introduced in 1989, followed by three in each of the following years.

SPECIALS

Over the years Lilliput Lane has been called upon to create cottages for special occasions or for individuals or groups of particularly valued customers. Examples include cottages just for club members, Christmas specials and commemorative issues for notable occasions such as the

annual collectors' banquet in South Bend, Indiana, each July and the collectors' fair held every summer in England.

Most of these cottages follow the usual Lilliput direction and are taken from real vernacular architecture still existing. Others are drawn from the popular 'after the vernacular' cottages copied by the Victorians and others from earlier styles.

Clockmakers, a Gothic Victorian gatehouse created by Lilliput Lane, is a good example of this movement. It represents a time when many famous architects —John Nash, P.F. Robinson, Repton, Voysey and others — designed picturesque cottages as a fashionable escape from the smoke and grime of the cities.

Some of the company's specials are ecclesiastical, others are vernacular farm buildings (Chiltern Mill, for example), but all have the Lilliput Lane touch, namely, a link with the past. The following section includes all of the specials created through July 1991.

Double Cottage

Jasmine Cottage

Oak Cottage

Sweet Briar Cottage

Rose Cottage

Diamond Cottage

Dial Cottage

Circular Cottage

Vine Cottage

Yuletide Inn

St. Nicholas Church

The Old Vicarage at Christmas

Deer Park Hall

Gulliver 1986

Bridge House Dealer Sign

Scroll on the Wall 1986

Cliburn School

Seven Dwarf's Cottage

The Guildhall

Izaak Waltons Cottage   Chantry Chapel

Mayflower House

Clockmaker's Cottage

Chiltern Mill

Olde York Toll

Bermuda Cottage Pink

Bermuda Cottage Blue

Bermuda Cottage Yellow

Rowan Lodge

Crendon Manor

210

Gardeners Cottage

Wenlock Rise

Yew Tree Farm

Bridle Way

Dovecot   *Puddlebrook*   *Little Lost Dog*

Wren Cottage   *Wishing Well*   *Lavender Cottage*

Packhorse Bridge 1987

Packhorse Bridge 1986

Cosy Corner

How th

Craftsn

ottages are Made

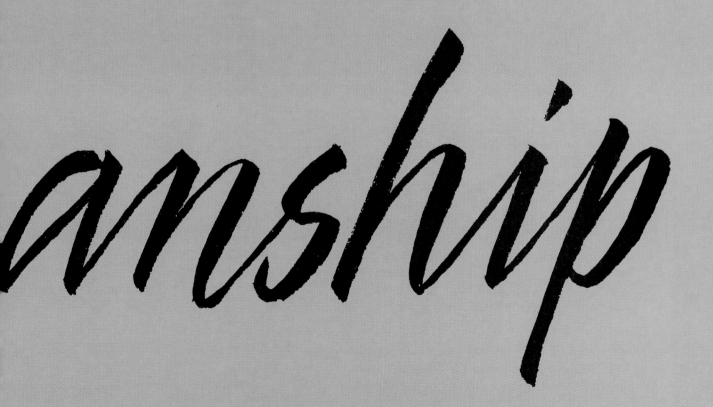

HOW THE COTTAGES ARE MADE

The making of a Lilliput Lane cottage involves an extraordinary combination of history, art and technology. A Lilliput Lane cottage represents a link between the past and the present, allowing the skills of those men who laboured to build the cottages long ago to be appreciated and enjoyed today. It is, fittingly, the artistic and technical skill of today's craftsmen and women at Lilliput Lane that make this possible. This is apparent in

Opposite:
Demoulding one of the very first casts of Saxham St. Edmunds

every process, from initial research, which ensures historical authenticity and integrity, to the artistry of the sculptors, the technical wizardry of tooling and casting and the patient precision of painting. Here we look at those skilled processes that bring Lilliput Lane cottages to life today.

RESEARCH

The most important decision in the whole
creative process of Lilliput Lane cottages
comes at the very beginning and concerns
which cottages are suitable to join Lilliput
Lane's range. David Tate and his team of
sculptors are constantly on the look-out for
cottages that capture the Lilliput Lane
spirit, and they travel thousands of miles a
year seeking out ideal examples, often
hidden away deep in the countryside. The
inspiration that sets them off on the track
may come from anywhere — perhaps a
cottage glimpsed on television, shown in a
magazine or, occasionally, photographed
by a collector. One of the most important
sources is Lilliput Lane's extensive archive
of books and reference material, and it is
to this that the sculptors turn to research
and authenticate their choices.

A Lilliput Lane cottage represents a
tiny slice of history, but it must do more
than this. It must capture the spirit and
charm of its time and of its surroundings
and invite people to share these delights.
Exactly what makes a cottage an ideal

*The paraphernalia of design surrounding the creation of
Paradise Lodge.*

subject for Lilliput Lane's miniaturisation is hard to define, but David Tate and the sculptors recognise that quality immediately. Proportion, style and integrity are essential features, but over-riding all these is a particular charm, a special magic that marks a cottage out from its neighbours. It may be the honesty with which it reveals its age through gentle weathering, or perhaps the quaint shape or angle of its thatch, or the endearing bulging of its walls, but more often it is a combination of many such features. Though there may be twenty pretty cottages in a village, usually only one or two have the qualities essential to Lilliput Lane.

Many photographs are taken of the cottage from every angle, and sketches made to capture the atmosphere and spirit of the place. Other buildings in the locality will also be recorded, to check that the cottage is truly authentic and typical of the area, rather than a 'one-off' copy imported from somewhere else. Integrity is all important at Lilliput Lane, and no cottage that is not what it seems, or deceives the eye in any way, has a place there.

Old reference material is consulted extensively, including Victorian photographs showing rural England as it was before widespread mechanisation changed the landscape. In the various local museums of architecture, the sculptors also gain valuable insights into how cottages were constructed, as well as about the techniques and materials that were used, whether wattle and daub or Devon cob.

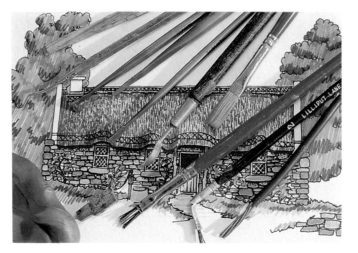

The drawing and tools that breathe life into the wax.

Opposite:
David Tate sketching in a remote valley in the Lake District National Park.

Sketching, painting, and taking photographs are essential to successful research.

This allows them to understand and portray the fabric of the building in greater and more accurate detail. It also means that where a cottage has suffered some later and inappropriate alteration or addition, the sculptors have a clear idea of its original appearance, and can portray it in its authentic state.

Once all the research has been completed, working drawings are made, showing the different views of the cottage, and including appropriate details. It is at this stage that any subtle changes are made, adjusting the proportions of the building to take account of the different perspective miniaturisation gives by putting less emphasis on the roof and more on the façade, and generally ensuring the most authentic appearance. Now all the plans are ready, and the sculpting process can begin.

SCULPTING

A Lilliput Lane cottage first takes shape in wax, though later it will pass through many stages in different materials. The wax used is made to a secret recipe specially formulated at Lilliput Lane for the purpose of sculpting cottages. It comprises different types of modelling wax mixed in carefully controlled proportions with other ingredients, which give it its unique properties. It is highly sensitive to temperature and can be quickly warmed and cooled. This is important, since some sculpting processes require the wax to be soft (making the original 'block'), and others, hard (all fine detailing).

Another significant feature is that the wax has little elastic 'memory'. This means that when a detail such as a window frame is impressed into its surface, the wax retains the impression without pushing out the other side, and it does not spring back when the tool is removed, as other malleable materials would.

Before sculpting can begin, the question of size and scale must be addressed. At Lilliput Lane there is an awareness that many of their pieces are likely to share a shelf together in a collector's home, and that their scale relative to each other is therefore important. On average, the scale

Soft, warm wax: the amorphous state that is the start of the real creative process.

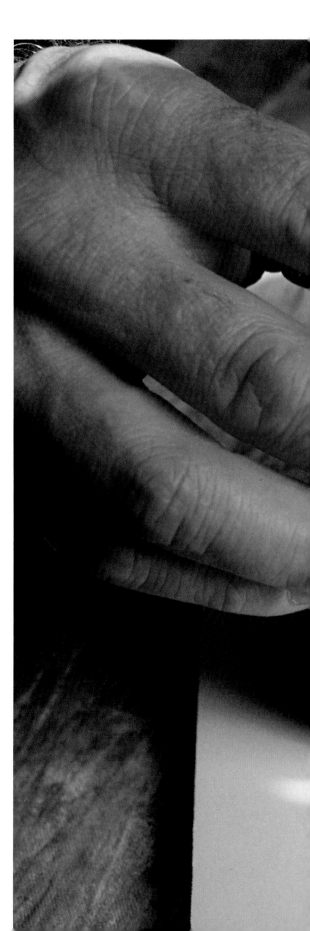

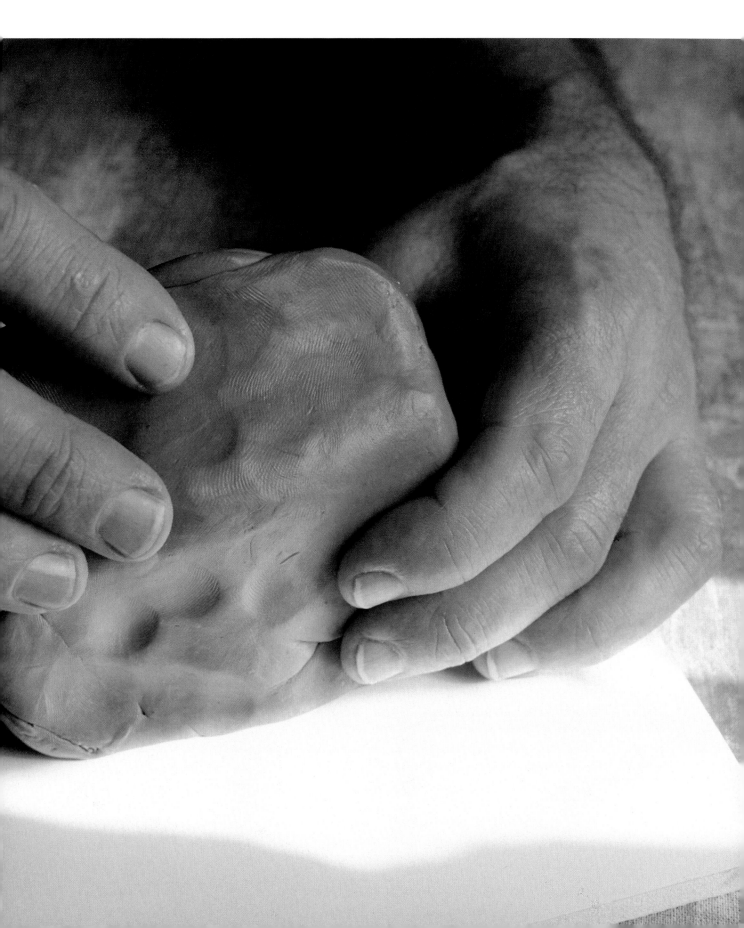

adopted is about 1/76 of real life, and the sculptors are now experienced enough to gauge relative scale, and thus size, by eye. Occasionally a particular piece may demand a shift in scale — for example, some of the Scottish castles, being buildings of a size exceptional to Lilliput Lane, are sculpted on a smaller scale than usual — but this is carefully judged.

The sculptors each have a set of nearly 200 tools that they have devised for the many intricate tasks involved in their work. While they find dental instruments useful, the sculptors are also highly innovative and create tools themselves specific to the task in hand, whether this is making individual flowers or creating particular textures — brickwork, grass and stone, for example. Thus bits of old wire brush, a radio aerial, pieces of wood, metal and perspex, as well as broken paintbrushes have all been pressed into active service in the hands of the sculptors. Many tools are specific to a particular cottage: for example, the blocks from which the windows are created, which are made of hardwood, pewter or perspex. These are individually created for each separate window, and

Opposite:
Fine detail is being added to a nearly complete wax of Hopcroft Cottage.

Skilled hands deftly mould a pug of soft warm wax to create the initial shape.

At work on a major introduction for 1992.

The painstakingly slow process of laying each tile one by one.

they may never be used again on another piece, since the shape or size will not be quite right.

It takes a sculptor a minimum of two weeks of uninterrupted and highly skilled work to create a finished wax of even the simplest cottage. More complex pieces take much longer (St Peter's Cove took over three months). All the way through the process the sculptors review and adjust their work. If they are not happy with it, the wax is forgiving and allows them to make modifications, though this becomes progressively more difficult. The sculptors take great pride in every piece they make, approaching it with total dedication and

always challenging themselves to surpass their previous 'best'. But they of all people are constantly made aware that they are part of a team, reliant on others for the final realisation of their work. No sooner have they completed their masterpiece than it is passed on to the tooling department for moulds and master copies to be made. Paradoxically, in being thus 'immortalised', it is itself destroyed, and the sculptors next see it as a mangled lump of wax, returned to them fit only for recycling.

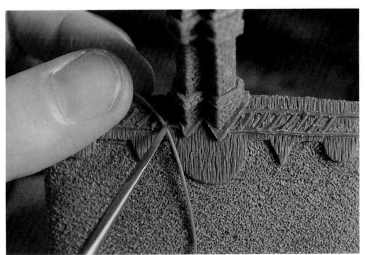

Stitching the thatch in wax.

The Old Shop at Bignor
Above: *Adding detail.*
Right: *Working on the thatch.*

Just some of the tools used to create the fine detail so special to Lilliput.

TOOLING AND MOULDING

At this stage, art meets technology to allow the single, original sculpture to be reproduced perfectly many times over. The technique of moulding employed at Lilliput Lane allows two apparently contradictory demands to be reconciled. The first is the need for the finest detail on a sculpted model to be reproduced faithfully, however complex. The second is the desire to keep costs down, to ensure that Lilliput Lane cottages reflect the best possible value for money. This means streamlining the production process while never compromising on quality, and it is David Tate's innovative and radical developments in mould-making that have made this possible.

The most significant feature of the moulding process at Lilliput Lane is that cottages are cast in one piece. This contrasts with the process used in reproducing complex shapes in porcelain, which involves moulding in several individual sections, according to form. The separate

Filling the master making moulds with a specially compounded epoxy resin, prior to loading into the Autoclave.

A glass reinforced plastic case is assembled around the master.

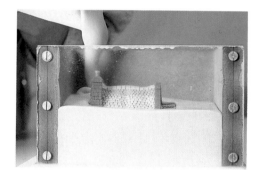

New wax disappears under silicone to create the first block mould.

A thin film of molten plastic material is built up layer by layer.

porcelain sections have to be joined together and fired. The key to avoiding this piecemeal process is the use of a highly flexible silicone elastomer mould, which allows casting in one piece and which can be gently eased off the cast once it has set hard. Much painstaking research has gone into the selection of a material suitable to this task, a material that can hold fine detail while remaining highly flexible and durable.

The use of such moulds is only possible because Lilliput Lane uses an extremely hard plaster, Amorphite instead of porcelain, that requires no firing or heat to set hard. It is this clever combination of silicone moulds and plaster, which crystallises at room temperature, that allows Lilliput Lane to circumvent several time-consuming and expensive processes and produce superb quality at fair prices.

The processes involved at this stage in production allow the creation of perfect images of the original wax sculpture, ready for painting and finishing. First of all, the

Setting the split line — a crucial stage.

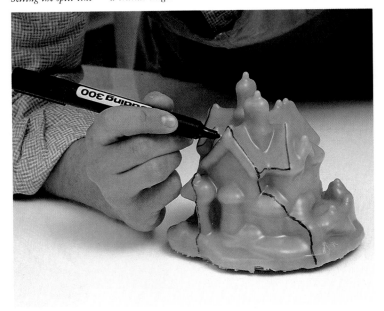

The three main components in a set of production equipment.

Vacuum Support Board.

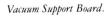

Silicone Back-up.

Silicone Mould.

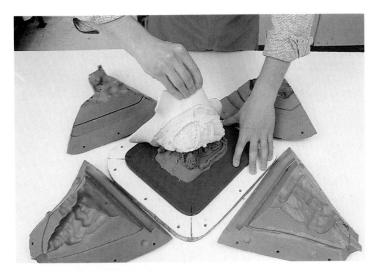

After the case has been fully removed the mould is carefully stripped from the master.

The first section to be removed from the case exposes the new mould.

Opposite:
Preparing equipment to measure impact strength on a batch of Amorphite®.

Filling a prototype mould with Amorphite in Pre-Production where new moulds and equipment are fully tested.

Carefully removing flashing and minor imperfections from a recently cast epoxy master.

Deep inside the master making mould of 'Victoriana'.

wax sculpture is passed to the Tooling Department. Here the 'tools' are developed from which the production mould systems and masters will be made. Tooling takes two to three months for each model, and involves over forty different processes and a variety of exotic materials, including cold-cured plastics, heat-cured polymers and thermoplastics.

Resin Casting is a separate yet integral part of the Tooling Department. Here epoxy masters are cast and put into an enormous, heated pressure vessel where the carefully formulated compounds are cured overnight. These masters are the fundamental cornerstone to the quality of the final casts.

After initial proving in Research and Development, the tools are passed to the Production Mould-Making Department where the final set of moulds and back-ups are made, tailored to each individual model. In the case of a new model, these then pass to the Pre-Production Department to prove their performance and potential. Otherwise moulds will normally go directly to the Casting Department.

In the Casting Department, the moulds are dipped in a wetting agent before the liquid Amorphite is carefully poured in. It takes a high degree of skill to fill a mould without trapping air, which would ruin the final cast. As the Amorphite is poured, the mould is vibrated to release air bubbles, and the casters take great care to ensure that the liquid has reached every tiny detail, down to the last flower petal.

When the Amorphite is beginning to set, the base of the cast is levelled, a process that is later completed by 'linishing' or grinding. Once the cast has cured, the process of demoulding begins. Great care and patience is required here to ease the mould off without snapping off a delicate chimney or spire.

While still 'green' (not completely hardened), the casts are passed to the

Quality Assurance is a keystone of the business. Here the supervisor closely examines a new master.

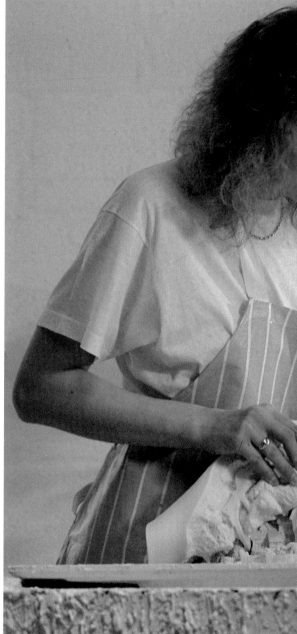

Fettling Department. Here the flashing — the thin slithers of plaster that remain in the deepest recesses of the model, such as bridges and tunnels — is removed. The casts are carefully inspected to ensure that every detail has been successfully moulded. After another 24-hour period of drying and hardening, they pass on for dipping.

Now in a semi-porous state, the cast is dipped into a mixture including polymers and pigments. This serves a dual purpose of sealing the surface and bringing out the detail by creating a marked contrast between different textures on the model. A series of different coloured dips may be used to build up a particular effect. The cast is then placed in the dehumidifying room for 48 hours to dry fully. One final inspection ensures that the dipping has had the desired effect, and the cast is ready for painting.

Pre-production casters demould the first casts of the Limited Edition — Saxham St. Edmunds.

PAINTING AND FINISHING

Here art takes over from science once more, as the cottages move on to the painting studios. Lilliput Lane employs over 300 painters, each of them fully trained in the meticulous skills required to breathe life into the cottages through the application of colour. The painters sit in small groups around a table sharing the paints placed in the centre on a specially designed rotating stand.

Painters each specialise in three or four different cottages, which allows them to paint as efficiently as possible. From the moment they start to paint a piece, until it is quite finished, they are entirely responsible for that piece, and on its merit they are judged. At no stage is work transferred between painters. With some models, a painter may paint more than one at the same time, applying each colour in turn. By the time that colour has been applied to the last piece, the first will be dry and ready to take the next colour. Larger, more complex models, however, will be painted individually, or in twos.

*A painter at work on a Limited Edition piece —
'Blair Atholl'.*

Talking through the finer points of colour and authenticity.

The painting process combines the individuality of the painters themselves with the need for absolute consistency of quality. The painters have a 'master' copy, to which they must match their own work to ensure consistency. But how they achieve this standard is up to them, and they all develop their own technique. Some prefer to paint the gardens first; others, the roofs. Throughout Lilliput Lane's history, these permanent, waterproof paints have regularly been revised and their formulas reworked. The new paint system introduced most recently has given Lilliput Lane's cottages renewed clarity and brilliance, and their intricately modelled gardens even more charm and authenticity.

Aware of the fascination painting holds for collectors of Lilliput Lane, the company regularly sends selected painters all over the world as its 'ambassadors'. Lilliput Lane's painters have travelled the United States, Japan and Australia, giving demonstrations of their skills. Anyone who has tried their own hand at painting a Lilliput Lane cottage at an open day will appreciate these artists' remarkable ability and patience.

Lilliput painters frequently appear at promotions around the world.

During colouration many options are looked at, notes on the base illustrate the different treatments and colours before the final choice is made.

A key asset to the success of Lilliput Lane is the enthusiasm of its people.

Tiny brushes for fine details.

In the Colouration Department, production masters receive their final touches before being issued to the painting studios.

Opposite:
*Careful packing assures that
the Collectors receive their
pieces in perfect condition.*

*Final inspection before Baiz-
ing and Packing.*

251

A Vis

Welc

Penrith

WELCOME TO LILILLIPUT LANE

Lilliput Lane has its home in Cumbria, an area of the far north-west of England renowned for the unique beauty of its scenery, where spectacular mountains and fells are riven by sparkling lakes amidst sylvan dales. At the heart of Cumbria is the Lake District, which can fairly lay claim to being the scenic jewel in England's crown. Its many attractions draw countless visitors, ranging from those seeking peaceful respite from the urban struggle

to those after the more energetic challenges that the mountains offer to walkers and climbers.

David Tate discovered the Lake District on a school trip from his native Yorkshire at the age of ten. He was smitten and in no time knew every peak, lake and fell. The romance blossomed, and at the age of fifteen, David was biking the ninety miles from his Yorkshire home for a weekend's climbing in the Lake District. Today, he is as keen as ever to share the delights of this magical area, and he encourages Lilliput Lane's visitors to explore for themselves.

Penrith, which is easily accessible by road or rail, stands at the northern gateway to the Lake District, so visitors to

Lilliput Lane are well placed to explore England's best-loved area. Just outside Penrith, off the Keswick road, are Lilliput Lane's original studios, occupying the old stables and outer houses of Skirsgill Park. While ten years ago any visitors would have found David Tate and his family busy at work in no more than a couple of small workshops, today they will find a highly organised complex spread over a much larger area. They will still, however, notice that the atmosphere is special, with teamwork, enthusiasm and dedication evident at every turn.

*Skirsgill scenes. Above left:
The original estate, still
occupied. To the right:
The stables, which now house
Lilliput's administrative
offices. Below: A Cumbrian
farmhouse.*

Through recent developments, Lilliput Lane can now offer its visitors the chance not only to see the many skilled processes that go into the production of the cottages but also to step back in time and see the company's past cottages, right back to the original examples made by David Tate at the very beginning. Standing in the middle of the cobbled courtyard, evoking a traditional English scene (complete with Victorian lamp-posts and old red telephone box), is Rose Cottage, where David first brought his family to live. As the cradle of Lilliput Lane, this simple building has been chosen and specially adapted to welcome collectors from

around the world. Here, they can enjoy seeing Lilliput Lane's cottages past and present, as well as learn about vernacular architecture.

Tours around the studios and workshops can be arranged for collectors by prior appointment, allowing them an insight into the time, effort and skill that goes into each and every Lilliput Lane cottage. They can then mull over what they have seen in the comfort of Gulliver's Pantry, where available refreshments range from a hearty meal to a good British cup of tea. Gulliver's Pantry has been created from the skilful conversion of the Skirsgill estate's old coach house, using massive old oak beams from a nearby building to keep the authentic rustic atmosphere. David Tate and his daughter Deborah have added to the charm by creating two beautiful windows in the 19th-century, Tiffany style, with vibrant stained-glass effects from resin colours on glass.

Having enjoyed a visit to Lilliput Lane itself, the visitor should take time to see the Lake District and the surrounding area, which have been such an inspiration to David Tate. Indeed, there is evidence that it inspired the whole concept of Lilliput, for the 18th-century author Jonathan Swift, in whose book, *Gulliver's Travels*, the miniature world of Lilliput Lane is first described, is reputed to have lived at Whitehaven, on the coast near here, as a child. It is said that the view from the windows of his house, high above the bay, of people and ships, all looking so tiny and distant, gave him the idea of a world in miniature, the world of Lilliput. Little did he know how long-lived his idea would be.

Jonathan Swift was by no means the only literary figure to have associations with this area. The great 19th-century English poet, William Wordsworth was born in Cockermouth and went to school in Penrith. As an adult he lived in Grasmere and Rydal, immortalising the beauties of the lakes in his poems and making his contemporaries aware of the romantic inspiration of this magical area. His visitors included his friend, Samuel Taylor Coleridge, as well as Sir Walter

David Tate chats with visitors from America.

257

Scott, Charlotte Brontë, Shelley and Keats, to name but a few. The surge of interest in this area that Wordsworth helped to generate in the 19th century left its mark on local architecture. The many buildings that the Victorians put up to accommodate the influx of visitors and settlers in the area are distinct from the original old farmsteads and cottages, yet they also make use of the local materials in their own particular style.

While two weeks could easily be whiled away in the Lake District, even a brief visit can encompass some of the magic it holds for the lover of vernacular architecture. The short route outlined below will give a flavour of the area as Lilliput Lane's original source of inspiration. As you stand on the doorstep of Lilliput Lane, nearby Penrith is the starting point.

Penrith is a thriving market town at the centre of a rich agricultural area. Its mellow red buildings, built of the local sandstone, line the streets that link its

innumerable marketplaces, each in its time reserved for selling particular produce. Penrith has had a colourful and turbulent history, being laid waste by the Scots in the Middle Ages, while prehistoric stones and monuments like King Arthur's Round Table (just south of Penrith) bear witness to the more distant past. History and legend meet in the churchyard, where the giant Torquin lies, supposedly killed by that most renowned Arthurian hero, Sir Lancelot du Lac.

Away from Penrith and up on the fells, is a land where traditionally there have been more sheep than people. Here the small farmhouses and cottages are made of the boulders and slate of the hills themselves, perched on the mountainside and braced against the vicissitudes of the weather. This represents the true vernacular tradition of the Lake District, and you must travel south-west from Penrith towards the lakes to see it at its best.

This route passes along the north-western shore of Ullswater, with wooded fells to one side and lake and mountain views to the other. This is where Wordsworth is reputed to have seen the 'host of golden daffodils' that inspired his famous poem, though the exact location is uncertain. Nonetheless, today in spring, this shore is ablaze with wild narcissi, quite as beautiful. Towards the south end of the lake, you pass through the villages of Glenridding (from which in summer a boat trip may be taken through the lake) and Patterdale (where the Victorian

church is known for the superb embroideries it houses). A brief diversion will bring you to the village of Hartsop, which is worth visiting for its 17th-century farm buildings and cottages, some of which have galleries on which the women would sit and spin wool. Then the road rises up to the mountains, bringing ever richer views of the high fells amidst wild and exposed mountain scenery.

Climbing up the Kirsktone Pass, you reach the highest road in the Lake District, thoughtfully provided with an inn, which must have been an especially welcome sight to travellers before motorised transport eased such ascents. A few miles further and an unmarked turning brings you down a perilously narrow and precipitous road into the village of Troutbeck. Here, 17th-and 18th-century cottages and farms cluster together around a

259

series of wells, with the old village school and the church, all much as they would have been centuries ago. The whole village is now a Conservation Area and is full of fascination for lovers of vernacular architecture. Perhaps most interesting of all, for those who have always wanted to 'see inside' their cottages, is Townend. This house was built by a yeoman farmer in 1626, and it is a typical example of Lakeland vernacular architecture, with its slate roof and cylindrical chimneys. It contains the original carved furniture, domestic utensils and papers of the family that occupied it for over 300 years. Now run by the National Trust, it is open to the public in the summer season.

A few miles away, along the shore of Lake Windermere, is Ambleside, well-known to Lilliput Lane collectors as the home of Bridge House, but with plenty of other good examples of vernacular architecture that should not be overlooked. Perched on its narrow stone bridge over Stock Ghyll, Bridge House is today owned by the National Trust and acts as an information centre, though the oven on the ground floor plus the upper storey still evoke its original domestic use. Near Bridge House and also of interest is an old watermill that was recently rebuilt, powered by the Stock Ghyll waterfall. Like many Lakeland towns, Ambleside has its own customs and gatherings — children carry rushes through the town in the annual Rushbearing Ceremony in July, and traditional Lakeland sports are held here in August.

Here, those with time to spare may decide to turn south to visit Near Sawrey on the edge of Esthwaite Water, to see Hill Top, the home of the famous children's author and illustrator, Beatrix Potter. Now open as a museum containing her furniture and belongings much as they would have been, this pretty 17th-century farmhouse was the inspiration for Lilliput Lane's Sawrey Gill. The picturesque village of

Rose Cottage, Skirsgill, where it all began.

North of Ambleside is Rydal, where Wordsworth lived later in his life. His home, Rydal Mount, is open in season, and contains family portraits, furniture and possessions. The gardens are as they were laid out by Wordsworth, and next to the house is Dora's Field, planted with daffodils and spectacular in spring. Two other homes in this area inspired Lilliput Lane's Rydal View and Stonybeck.

The road takes you along the north shore of Rydal Water, a small prettily wooded lake, to Grasmere. Wordsworth's most famous home is here, Dove Cottage, which has been depicted by Lilliput Lane. Once a pub called the Dove and Olive Branch, it now enjoys a sedate existence as a place of pilgrimage, and with its neighbouring museum, it is open all year round. Incidentally, just next door to Dove Cottage is a cottage bearing fine examples of the cylindrical chimneys so peculiar to Lakeland. Near here, to the west of the road sits a little holiday cottage that was the inspiration for Helmere.

A spectacular drive up over Dunmail Raise, which affords superb mountain views, brings you to Thirlmere. The lake was greatly expanded at the end of the 19th century to create a reservoir for

261

Hawkshead, nearby, is also worth visiting with its whitewashed buildings and slate roofs. Just north of here is 15th-century Hawkshead Courthouse, now a museum of local rural life, with displays on coppicing, charcoal-burning, the local iron industry and fishing for Windermere char, a fish unique to this lake.

A nearby bridge house that inspired a cottage of the same name. Right, a street scene in Penrith, a market town for the surrounding area.

Narrow passageways or 'ginnels' run between the buildings (some little more than 18 inches wide), and many an ancient inn is tucked away there. In the centre is the strangely church-like town hall, showing the influence of German heritage, a legacy of Elizabethan times when German miners were brought into the area.

From Keswick, those with time can bear westwards to visit Cockermouth, an ancient market town that was the chief commercial centre in the old county of Cumberland, back in the 17th century. Today, it retains much of its original character and is known chiefly to visitors for another Wordsworth connection, the house where the poet was born, which is open to the public and gives a glimpse of late 18th-century life. Domestic Georgian architecture and early industrial buildings combine easily in Cockermouth (and of course today it is also home to one of Lilliput Lane's studios), and there is plenty to interest a visitor.

Returning eastwards, Lilliput Lane collectors should also visit the Eden Valley, the other side of Penrith, not just to see St Lawrence's Church in Crosby Ravensworth, but to enjoy this little known area. David Tate calls this area 'the land time forgot' — its distant past lost in the myth and legend of ancient stone circles

Manchester, and sadly two old villages were submerged, with only the 17th-century church from one of them remaining at Wythburn. Passing on, over Nest Brow you see a panoramic view of the little grey town of Keswick, the 'capital' of the northern Lake District, which huddles between Derwentwater and Bassenthwaite, at the foot of the majestic mountain of Skiddaw. Keswick today is an attractive, welcoming town of tightly packed grey houses, with some of the grandest examples of Victorian architecture in the area.

Scenes from Penrith. Visitors can roam in every direction from Lilliput Lane and find a quiet charm in the region's picturesque villages and countryside.

like Long Meg and her daughters, its present an unspoilt land of red sandstone bridges and quiet villages, each with its own customs and festivals. With tourists invariably drawn to the lakes and peaks, few venture to this secret valley of more subtle charms, to see life unchanged and undisturbed by the demands of tourism.

As well as walking, climbing and sight-seeing, Cumbria offers countless opportunities to enjoy the traditional annual festivals and gatherings that occur in different villages throughout the year. June sees the notorious horsefair at Appleby-in-Westmorland, the last of the real Romany horsefairs that is informally described as 'a wild affair of galloping horses and drunkenness' — only for the brave.

The Grasmere Sports is the most famous of the traditional sports events, and occurs in August. Among the day's events is Westmorland and Cumberland wrestling, with its own peculiar set of rules, not to mention even more peculiar clothing of vest and long-johns beneath colourful trunks. Fell racing is another local sport, in which the seriously fit run up a mountain and down the other side in just a few minutes — a distance and gradient it would take most of us two hours to cover.

Finally, those with an interest in the old industries of the area that have had so

much bearing on its history, from the slate to coal to wool, should visit the Museum of Lakeland Life and Industry in Kendal. Here there are reconstructed workshops and farmhouse rooms evoking the Lakeland past.

Even the briefest of visits cannot fail to impress upon the visitor the charms of this unique and varied area, which combines the magic of the past with abundant opportunities for enjoyment today and so much potential for the future. It is no surprise then that David Tate, with his love of the outdoor life, and his boundless enthusiasm for the landscape and its heritage, chose Cumbria as the cradle of his Lilliput dream.

INTRODUCTION TO INDEX

T his index is arranged alphabetically. It includes: a two-letter designation for region or country (see below), height in inches and centimeters, date of introduction and (where applicable) retirement, and footnotes. The latter applies only to cottages that have special information of interest to collectors. Finally, there is a page reference for locating cottages in this book.

Although there are 18 official vernacular divisions within Great Britain, they have been amalgamated into six areas.

These are:

(SE) – South-East England
Including East Anglia and the Home Counties.

(SW) – South-West England
Including Southern Cotswold/Limestone Belt.

(MI) – Midlands
Including East and West Midlands, and adjoining Cotswold/Limestone Belt.

(NC) – North of England and Cumbria
Including South Pennines, North-west England, Cumbria, Yorkshire Dales, East Yorkshire and Humberside, and North-east England

(SC) – Scotland

(WA) – Wales

Other countries are: Ireland (IR), France (FR), Germany (GE), the Netherlands (NL), and the United States (US).

The First American Collection (US1) was introduced in October 1984 and retired in October 1985. The American Landmarks Collection (US2) began in 1989. At press time, two cottages —Pepsi Cola Barn and Pioneer Barn —were scheduled for retirement at the end of 1991.

Retirement dates for all Club pieces are for the U.K. chapter. The appropriate dates for the U.S. chapter are approximately two months later.

The symbol (*) denotes no region or country designation.

COLLECTORS' INDEX

COLLECTORS' INDEX

COLLECTORS' INDEX

COLLECTORS' INDEX

FOOTNOTES TO INDEX

1. Acorn Cottage — Several minor alterations were made prior to a major renovation in September 1983, which was then retired in December 1987.
2. April Cottage — Minor alterations were made prior to July 1984. This revised model was then retired in December 1989.
3. Coach House — Crosses were removed from beneath the eaves in December 1982.
4. The Croft — Sheep were added in July 1984.
5. Dale Farm — Windows were replaced prior to a major renovation in September 1983.
6. Dale House — Given new windows in September 1983.
7. Drapers — Original had red tiled roof, later changed to grey/green.
8. Honeysuckle — Prior to a major renovation in December 1983, up to five minor changes were made. Very early pieces included honey coloured dog.
9. Lakeside House — Several windows were removed in February 1983.
10. Oak Lodge — Several minor changes were made prior to renovation in September 1983.
11. Old Mine — Only 200 pieces made.
12. Stone Cottage — Front nameplate removed in September 1983.
13. Sussex Mill — Two minor renovations were made prior to a major change in July 1984.
14. Castle Street — Was out of production for six months during 1984.
15. Holly Cottage — Slight changes made prior to major renovation in July 1984.
16. Anne Hathaway's Cottage — Front nameplate removed plus other minor alterations in September 1983.
17. Dove Cottage — Front nameplate removed in September 1983.
18. Miners — Underwent colour changes which included roof and door in September 1983.
19. Wm. Shakespeare's Birthplace — Front nameplate removed in September 1983.
20. Warwick Hall — Front nameplate removed. Other alterations made in September 1983.
21. Cliburn School — Only 62 made. Special Edition to commemorate 1860-1983.
22. Preston Mill — New pan tiles and waterwheel in December 1986.
23. Bronte Parsonage — Window frames thickened during first month of production.
24. Hermitage — Piece enlarged, garden shed added, flowers added in December 1986.
25. Kentish Oast House — Plastic cowl replaced metal cowl in December 1986.
26. Bermuda Cottage — Exclusive to Bermuda market, available in three colours.
27. Three Feathers — Sign changed in April 1986.
28. Packhorse Bridge — Collectors Club Gift. North American version also produced — shield different.
29. Crendon Manor — Collectors Club numbered Limited Edition of 1500.
30. Little Lost Dog — Collectors Club Gift. Altered on two occasions, therefore three variations were issued.
31. Guildhall — Exclusive to Guild members in UK.
32. Inglewood — Windows sharpened in December 1989.
33. Izaak Walton's Cottage — Exclusive to Church's China in UK for first 12 months.
34. Clockmaker's Cottage — Exclusive to H Samuels in UK.
35. Yew Tree Farm — Collectors Club Special Edition —exclusive for year of issue.
36. Wishing Well — Collectors Club Gift.
37. Deer Park Hall — Christmas Special 1988/89.
38. Wenlock Rise — Collectors Club Special Edition —exclusive for year of issue.
39. Chantry Chapel — Exclusive to Peter Jones China in UK.
40. Chine Cot — Four windows removed, remainder replaced. Doors re-styled in December 1989.
41. Saint Peter's Cove — Limited Edition of 3000 — numbered.
42. Dovecot — Collectors Club Gift.
43. Mayflower House — Exclusive to USA.
44. Blair Atholl — Limited Edition of 3000 — numbered.
45. Chiltern Mill — Exclusive to H Samuels in UK, openly available in USA.
46. Lavender Cottage — Collectors Club Special Edition —exclusive for year of issue.
47. Saint Nicholas Church — Christmas Special 1989/90.
48. Mrs. Pinkerton's Post Office — Exclusive to Guild members in UK, openly available in USA. From July 1991 — general worldwide release.
49. Olde York Toll — Exclusive to Peter Jones China in UK, openly available in USA.
50. Cawdor Castle — Limited Edition of 3000 — numbered.
51. Sulgrave Manor — Exclusive to Church's China in UK, openly available in USA. From July 1991 — general release worldwide.
52. Bridle Way — Collectors Club Special Edition — exclusive for year of issue.
53. Cosy Corner — Collectors Club Gift.
54. Rowan Lodge — Exclusive to Lilliput special events. 350 produced for 1990 South Bend Show, USA, with different coloured roof.
55. Yuletide Inn — Christmas Special 1990/91.
56. Gardeners Cottage — Collectors Club Special Edition — exclusive for year of issue.
57. Puddlebrook — Collectors Club Gift —exclusive for year of issue.
58. Seven Dwarfs Cottage — Only 470 produced. Exclusive to USA.
59. Saxham St. Edmunds — Limited Edition 4500 worldwide.
60. Victoriana (American Landmarks) — Limited Edition 2500.
61. The Old Vicarage at Christmas — Christmas Special 1991.
62. Gamekeepers Cottage — Replaces Rowan Lodge as special for events only. 350 produced for South Bend Show 1991, USA, with different roof colour.
63. Wren Cottage — Collectors Club Special. Member-get-a-Member programme 1991.
64. First American Collection — Total pieces produced: Adobe Church — 475; Adobe Village —225; Cape Cod Cottage —225; Country Church — 500; Forge Barn —275; Grist Mill — 150; General Store —150 (sign was changed during production); Lighthouse — 200; Log Cabin —150 (two versions); Midwest Barn — 400; San Francisco — 400; Wallace Station —150; Covered Bridge — No record.